EARLIER AMERICAN MUSIC

Edited by H. Wiley Hitchcock
for the *Music Library Association*

9

THE AMERICAN
MUSICAL MISCELLANY

THE AMERICAN MUSICAL MISCELLANY

A Collection of the Newest and Most Approved Songs,
Set to Music

NEW INTRODUCTION BY H. WILEY HITCHCOCK

Director, Institute for Studies in American Music,
Brooklyn College, CUNY

DA CAPO PRESS • NEW YORK • 1972

Library of Congress Catalog Card Number 75-39731

ISBN 0-306-77309-0

Published by Da Capo Press, Inc.
A Subsidiary of Plenum Publishing Corporation
227 West 17th Street, New York, New York 10011

EDITOR'S FOREWORD

American musical culture, from Colonial and Federal Era days on, has been reflected in an astonishing production of printed music of all kinds: by 1820, for instance, more than fifteen thousand musical publications had issued from American presses. Fads, fashions, and tastes have changed so rapidly in our history, however, that comparatively little earlier American music has remained in print. On the other hand, the past few decades have seen an explosion of interest in earlier American culture, including earlier American music. College and university courses in American civilization and American music have proliferated; recording companies have found a surprising response to earlier American composers and their music; a wave of interest in folk and popular music of past eras has opened up byways of musical experience unimagined only a short time ago.

It seems an opportune moment, therefore, to make available for study and enjoyment—and as an aid to furthering performance of earlier American music —works of significance that exist today only in a few scattered copies of publications long out of print, and works that may be well known only in later editions or arrangements having little relationship to the original compositions.

Earlier American Music is planned around several types of musical scores to be reprinted from early editions of the eighteenth, nineteenth, and early twentieth centuries. The categories are as follows:

Songs and other solo vocal music
Choral music and part-songs
Solo keyboard music
Chamber music
Orchestral music and concertos
Dance music and marches for band
Theater music

The idea of *Earlier American Music* originated in a paper read before the Music Library Association in February, 1968, and published under the title "A Monumenta Americana?" in the Association's journal, *Notes* (September, 1968). It seems most appropriate, therefore, for the Music Library Association to sponsor this series. We hope *Earlier American Music* will stimulate further study and performance of musical Americana.

H. Wiley Hitchcock

INTRODUCTION

The American Musical Miscellany resembles in form and function one of the most popular types of Federal-era publication: the pocket songster, some five hundred different versions of which were issued before 1820. But the typical songster included only the texts of the songs it contained; the music, if mentioned at all, was indicated only by the name of the tune. *The American Musical Miscellany,* on the other hand, includes music for every one of its more than one hundred songs—the melody alone for sixty-nine, more elaborate music for the rest. It is also an exceptionally large collection. Thus it is an especially valuable and revealing index of New England's taste in song in the 1790's.

We do not know who compiled the book, nor who was the "able master" (mentioned in its preface) employed "to inspect and correct the music." Their aims were "to cull, from a great variety of ancient songs, such as have been, at all times, generally approved"; to add to these the "newest songs"; and, finally, to emphasize "American productions." (An advertisement for the volume, placed in Boston's *Columbian Centinel* in February, 1799, made a special point of mentioning the "large variety of the late Federal American songs, suited to the spirit of the times.") Thus we find English, Scottish, and Irish songs as well as Revolutionary and Federal songs; songs of the sea and of the forest; drinking songs and temperance songs; songs about the Indian and about the Negro; songs of the hearth and songs of the ballad-opera stage; anonymous folkish songs and songs whose composers we can identify. The compilers exercised a certain genteel selectivity: they "endeavoured to avoid such as would give offence to the delicate ear of chastity itself." Thus the musical picture projected in *The American Musical Miscellany* is not wholly a rounded one. Even so, the collection mirrors the variety and the vitality of secular song in post-Revolutionary War America.

H.W.H.

THE AMERICAN
MUSICAL MISCELLANY

THE

American Musical Miscellany:

A

COLLECTION

OF THE NEWEST AND MOST APPROVED

SONGS,

SET TO MUSIC.

'Tis thine, sweet power, to raise the thought sublime,
Quell each rude passion, and the heart refine.
Soft are thy strains as Gabriel's gentlest string,
Mild as the breathing zephyrs of the spring.
Thy pleasing influence, thrilling thro' the breast,
Can lull e'en raging anguish into rest.
And oft thy wildly sweet enchanting lay,
To fancy's magick heaven steals the rapt thought away.

PRINTED AT NORTHAMPTON, Massachusetts.

BY ANDREW WRIGHT,

For DANIEL WRIGHT and COMPANY.

Sold by them, and by S. BUTLER, in Northampton ; by I. THOMAS,
Jun. in Worcester ; by F. BARKER, in Greenfield : and by
the principal booksellers in Boston.—1798.

TO

ALL TRUE LOVERS

OF

S O N G,

IN THE

UNITED STATES OF *COLUMBIA*,

THIS *VOLUME*,

IS HUMBLY DEDICATED,

By their friends

and humble

servants,

THE PUBLISHERS.

TO THE PUBLIC.

THE *Editors* of the AMERICAN MUSICAL MISCELLANY, present the public with the following collection of *Songs*, accompanied with *notes :*—And whenever they have found the same words of a song sung in different tunes, (which is not unfrequently the case) they have endeavoured to felect such notes as, in their opinion, were best adapted to the words ; but whether they have, in every instance, been happy in the selections, will be determined by the connoisseurs in the science of MUSIC. Great care has been taken that the work should be accurate ; and an able mafter employed to inspect and correct the MUSIC. The great proficiency which, within a few years past, has been made in

A 2

the various branches of this science, and the facility with which the lovers cf MU-SIC, now read notes to which they have not been accustomed, has induced the Editors to believe that this work would at leaft be acceptable to the public.

Their aim has been to cull, from a great variety of ancient SONGS, such as have been, at all times, generally approved ; and have endeavoured to avoid such as would give offence to the delicate ear of chastity itself.—A general preference has been given to American productions, and perhaps nothing will more effectually exhibit the progress of the human mind in the refinements which characterize the age, than the songs, which from general consent, are now in vogue.

CONTENTS.

viii CONTENTS.

CONTENTS.

CONTENTS.

CONTENTS.

W

American Musical Miscellany.

BEING A COLLECTION OF THE MOST APPROVED SONGS AND
AIRS, BOTH OLD AND NEW.

SONG I.

THE LUCKY ESCAPE.

I that once was a ploughman, a sailor am
now. No lark that a-loft in the sky, Ever flutter'd his wings to give speed to the plough Was
so gay and so carelefs as I, Was so gay and
so carelefs as I; But my friend was a car-

B

findo-aboard a king's ship, And he ax'd me to.

go just to sea for a trip; And he talk'd of such

things as if sailors were kings, And so teazing did

keep, and so teazing did keep, That I left my poor

plough to go ploughing the deep. No long-er the

horn call'd me up in the morn, No longer the

horn call'd me up in the morn, I trusted the

carfindo and the inconstant wind, That made me

for to go and leave my dear be-hind.

I did not much like for to be aboard a fhip.
   When in danger there is no door to creep out;
I liked the jolly tars, I liked bumbo and flip,
   But I did not like rocking about;

By and by came a hurricane, I did not like that,
Next a battle that many a failor laid flat;
      Ah! cried I, who would roam,
      That like me had a home;
      When I'd fow and I'd reap,
Ere I left my poor plough, to go ploughing the deep,
      Where fweetly the horn
      Call'd me up in the morn,
Ere I trufted the Carfindo and the inconftant wind,
That made me for to go and leave my dear behind.

At laft fafe I landed, and in a whole fkin,
   Nor did I make any long ftay,
Ere I found by a friend who I ax'd for my kin,
   Father dead, and my wife run away!
Ah who but thyfelf, faid I, haft thou to blame?
Wives loofing their hufbands oft lofe their good name.
      Ah why did I roam
      When fo happy at home:
      I could fow and could reap,
Ere I left my poor plough to go ploughing the deep:

When so sweetly the horn
Call'd me up in the morn,
Curse light upon the Carsindo and inconstant wind,
That made me for to go and leave my dear behind.

Why if that be the case, said this very same friend,
    And you ben't no more minded to roam,
Gi'e's a shake by the fist, all your care's at an end,
    Dad's alive and your wife's safe at home.
Stark staring with joy, I leapt out of my skin,
Buss'd my wife, mother, sister, and all of my kin:
        Now, cried I, let them roam,
        Who want a good home,
        I am well, so I'll keep,
Nor again leave my plough to go ploughing the deep;
        Once more shall the horn
        Call me up in the morn,
Nor shall any damn'd Carsindo, nor the inconstant wind,
E'er tempt me for to go and leave my dear behind.

SONG II.

THE FLOWING CAN.

A failor's life's a life of woe, He works

now late now early; Now up and down, now

to and fro, What then? he takes it cheerly.

Bleft with a fmiling can of grog, If duty call,

ftand, rife, or fall, To fates laft verge he'll jog.

The kedge to weigh, the fheets belay, He does

B 2

it with a wish, To heave the lead, or to cat-

head the pond'rous anchor fish: For while the

grog goes round, All sense of danger's drown'd,

We despise it to a man. We sing a little, And

laugh a little, And work a little, And swear a

little: We sing a little, And laugh a little, And

work a little, And swear a little: And fiddle a

little, And foot it a little, And swig the flowing

can, And fiddle a little, And foot it a little,

And ſwig the flowing can, And ſwig the flow-

ing can, And ſwig the flowing can.

If howling winds and roaring ſeas
  Give proof of coming danger,
We view the ſtorm, our hearts at eaſe,
  For Jack's to fear a ſtranger.
Bleſt with the ſmiling grog, we fly
    Where now below
    We headlong go,
Now riſe on mountains high :
    Spight of the gale,
    We hand the ſail,
Or take the needful reef ;
    Or man the deck,
    To clear ſome wreck,
To give the ſhip relief.

Though perils threat around,
All ſenſe of danger's drown'd,
We deſpiſe it to a man.
    We ſing a little, &c.

But yet think not our cafe is hard,
 Though ftorms at fea thus treat us,
For coming home,--a fweet reward,
 With fmiles our fweethearts greet us.
Now too the friendly grog we quaff,
  Our am'rous toaft,
  Her we love moft,
And gayly fing and laugh,
  The fails we furl,
  Then for each girl,
The petticoat difplay.
  The deck we clear,
  Then three times cheer,
As we their charms furvey.
And then the grog goes round,
All fenfe of danger's drown'd,
We defpife it to a man.
  We fing a little, &c.

SONG III.

ALLOA HOUSE.

The spring time re-turns, and cloaths the

green plains, And Alloa shines more cheerful

and gay; The lark tunes his throat, and the

neighbouring swains sing merrily round me where-

ev-er I stray; But San-dy no more re-

turns to my view! No spring time me cheers,

no mu-fic can charm, He's gone, and I fear

me for-ev-er a-dieu! A-dieu, ev'ry pleafure

this bo-fom can warm!

O Alloa houfe! how much art thou chang'd!
How filent, how dull to me is each grove!
Alone I here wander where once we both rang'd,
Alas! where to pleafe me my Sandy once ftrove!

Here Sandy I heard the tales that you told;
Here liftened too fond, whenever you fung;
Am I grown lefs fair, then, that you are turn'd cold?
Or foolifh, believ'd a falfe, flattering tongue;

So fpoke the fair maid; when forrow's keen pain,
And fhame, her laft fault'ring accents fuppreft:
For fate at that moment brought back her dear fwain.
Who heard, and, with rapture, his Nelly addreft:
My Nelly! my fair, I come; O my Love,
No power fhall thee tear again from my arm,
And, Nelly! no more thy fond fhepherd reprove,
Who knows thy fair worth, and adores all thy charms.

She heard ; and new joy fhot thro' her foft frame,
And will you, my love ! be true ? fhe reply 'd,
And live I to meet my fond fhepherd the fame ?
Or dream I that Sandy will make me his bride ?
O Nelly ! I live to find thee ftill kind ;
Still true to thy fwain, and lovely as true ;
Then adieu ! to all forrow : what foul is fo blind
As not to live happy for ever with you !

SONG IV.

THE DUSKY NIGHT.

The dufky night rides down the fky, And

ufhers in the morn ; The hounds all join in jo-

vial cry, The hounds all join in jovial cry, The

huntfman winds his horn, The huntfman winds

his horn. And a hunting we will go,   A hunt-

ing we will go,   A hunting we will go - - -

A hunting we will go. And a hunting we will

go,   A hunting we will go, And hunting we

will go - - A hunting we will go.

The wife around her hufband throws
   Her arms to make him ftay :
My dear, it rains, it hails, it blows,
   You cannot hunt to day.
      Yet a hunting, &c.

Sly Reynard now like light'ning flies,
   And fweeps acrofs the vale ;

But when the hounds too near he ſpies,
  He drops his buſhy tail.
    Then a hunting, &c.

Fond echo ſeems to like the ſport,
  And join the jovial cry ;
The woods and hills the ſound retort,
  And muſic fills the ſky,
    When a hunting, &c.

At laſt his ſtrength to faintneſs worn,
  Poor Reynard ceaſes flight ;
Then hungry homeward we return
  To feaſt away the night.
    And a drinking, &c.

Ye jovial hunters in the morn
  Prepare then for the chaſe ;
Riſe at the ſounding of the horn,
  And health with ſport embrace,
    When a hunting, &c.

C

SONG V.

PLATO's ADVICE.

Says Pla-to, why should man be vain? Since

bounteous heaven has made him great; Why

looketh he with insolent disdain On those un-

deck'd with wealth or state? Can splendid robes,

or beds of down, Or costly gems that deck

the fair; Can all the glo - - - - - - - - - - -

- - - - - - - - - - - - - - - - - - - ries of a crown,

Give health, or eafe the brow of care?

The fcepter'd king, the burthen'd flave,
 The humble, and the haughty, die ;
The rich, the poor, the bafe, the brave,
 In duft, without diftinction, lie.
Go fearch the tombs where monarchs reft,
 Who once the greateft titles bore :
The wealth and glory they poffefs'd,
 And all their honours, are no more.

So glides the meteor thro' the fky,
 And fpreads along a gilded train ;
But when its fhort-liv'd beauties die,
 Diffolves to commom air again.
So 'tis with us, my jovial fouls !—
 Let friendfhip reign while here we ftay ;
Let's crown our joys with flowing bowls—
 When Jove us calls we muft away.

SONG VI.

THE ECHOING HORN.

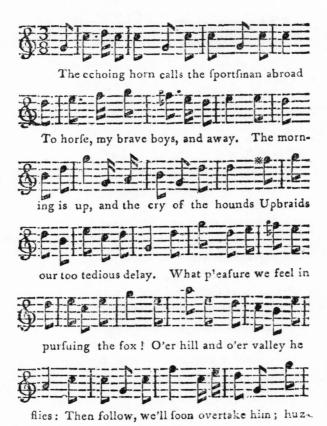

The echoing horn calls the sportsman abroad

To horse, my brave boys, and away.   The morn-

ing is up, and the cry of the hounds Upbraids

our too tedious delay.   What pleasure we feel in

pursuing the fox ! O'er hill and o'er valley he

flies : Then follow, we'll soon overtake him ; huz-

za! The traitor is feiz'd on and dies. He dies - -

- - - - - - - - - - - - - - The traitor is feiz'd on

Chorus.

and dies. Then follow, we'll foon overtake him,

huzza! The traitor is feiz'd on, and dies.

Triumphant returning at night with the fpoil,
   Like Bacchanals, fhouting and gay;
How fweet with a bottle and lafs to refrefh,
   And drown the fatigues of the day!
With fport, love, and wine, fickle fortune defy;
   Dull wifdom all happinefs fours.
Since life is no more than a paffage at beft,
   Let's ftrew the way over with flow'rs.
   With flow'rs; lets ftrew, &c.

SONG VII.

QUEEN MARY's FAREWELL TO FRANCE.

O ! thou lov'd country, where my youth was

spent, Dear golden days, All paſt in ſweet con-

tent, Where the fair morning of my clouded day

Shone mildly bright, and temperately gay. Dear

France, adieu, a long and ſad farewell ! No thought

can image, and no tongue can tell, The pangs

I feel at that drear word—farewell !

The ship that wafts me from thy friendly shore,
Conveys my body, but conveys no more.
My soul is thine, that spark of heav'nly flame,
That better portion of my mingled frame,
Is wholly thine, that part I give to thee,
That in the temple of thy memory,
The other ever may enshrined be.

SONG VIII.

POOR TOM, OR THE SAILOR's EPITAPH.

Here, a sheer hulk, lies poor Tom Bow_

ling, The darling of our crew ; No more

he'll hear the tempest howling, For death

has broach'd him to. His form was of

the manliest beauty, His heart was kind and

soft ; Faithful below he did his du-ty,

And now he's gone a ----loft, And now

he's gone a --- loft.

Tom never from his word departed,
　　His virtues were so rare,
His friends were many, and true-hearted,
　　His Poll was kind and fair :
And then he'd sing so blithe and jolly,
　　Ah many's the time and oft !
But mirth is turn'd to melancholy,
　　For Tom is gone aloft.

1

Yet fhall Poor Tom find pleafant weather,
 When he who all commands,
Shall give, to call life's crew together,
 The word to pipe all hands.
Thus death, who kings and tars difpatches,
 In vain Tom's life has doff'd ;
For, tho' his body's under hatches,
 His foul is gone aloft.

SONG IX.

NEVER TILL NOW I KNEW LOVE'S SMART.

Never till now I knew love's fmart, Guefs who

it was that ftole away my heart ? 'Twas on-ly

you, if you'll believe me, 'Twas only you if

you'll believe me.

Since that I've felt love's fatal pow'r,
Heavy has pafs'd each anxious hour,
If not with you, if you'll believe me,
    If not with you, &c.

Honour and wealth no joys can bring,
Nor I be happy tho' a king,
If not with you, if you'll believe me,
    If not with you, &c.

When from this world I'm call'd away,
For you alone I'd wifh to ftay,
For you alone, if you'll believe me,
    For you alone, &c.

Grave on my tomb, where'er I'am laid,
Here lies one who lov'd but one maid,
That's only you, if you'll believe me.
    That's only you, &c.

SONG X.

THE BANKS OF THE DEE.

'Twas fummer, and foftly the breezes were

blowing, And fweetly the nightingale fung from

the tree ; At the foot of a rock where the river

was flowing, I fat myfelf down on the banks

of the Dee. Flow on, lovely Dee, flow on thou

fweet river, Thy banks, pureft ftream, fhall be

dear to me ever : For there I firft gain'd the

affection and favour Of Ja - mie the glory and

pride of the Dee.

But now he's gone from me, and left me thus mourn-
    ing,
To quell the proud rebels—for valiant is he ;
And ah ! there's no hopes of his fpeedy returning,
To wander again on the Banks of the Dee.
He's gone, haplefs youth, o'er the loud-roaring bil-
    lows,
The kindeft and fweeteft of all the gay fellows,
And left me to ftray 'mongft the once loved willows,
The lonelieft maid on the Banks of the Dee.

But time and my prayers may perhaps yet reftore
    him,
Bleft peace may reftore my dear fhepherd to me ;
And when he returns, with fuch care I'll watch
    o'er him,
He never fhall leave the fweet Banks of the Dee.
The Dee then fhall flow, all its beauties difplaying ;
The lambs on its banks fhall again be feen playing ;
While I, with my Jamie, am carelefsly ftraying,
And tafting again all the fweets of the Dee.

ADDITIONS BY A LADY.

Thus fung the fair maid on the banks of the river,
And fweetly re-echo'd each neighbouring tree ;
But now all thefe hopes muft evanifh for ever,
Since Jamie fhall ne'er fee the Banks of the Dee.

On a foreign fhore the fweet youth lay dying,
In a foreign grave his body's now lying ;
While friends and acquaintance in Scotland are
    crying
For Jamie the glory and pride of the Dee.

  Mis-hap on the hand by whom he was wounded ;
Mis-hap on the wars that call'd him away   (ed,
From a circle of friends by which he was furround-
Who mourn for dear Jamie the tedious day.
Oh ! poor haplefs maid, who mourns difcontented,
The lofs of a lover fo juftly lamented ;
By time, only time, can her grief be contented,
And all her dull hours become cheerful and gay.

  Twas honour and brav'ry made him leave her
    mourning,
From unjuft rebellion his country to free ;
He left her in hopes of a fpeedy returning,
To wander again on the Banks of the Dee.
For this he defpifed all dangers and perils ;
'Twas thus he efpoufed Britannia's quarrels,
That when he came home he might crown her with
    laurels,
The happieft maid on the Banks of the Dee.

  But fate had determin'd his fall to be glorious,
Tho' dreadful the thought muft be unto me ;
      D

He fell, like brave Wolfe, when the troops were
    victorious ;
Sure each tender heart muft bewail the decree :
Yet, tho' he is gone, the once faithful lover,
And all our fine fchemes of true happinefs over,
No doubt he implored his pity and favour
For me he had left on the Banks of the Dee.

SONG XI.

THE HEAVY HOURS.

The heavy hours are almoft paft That part

my love and me ; My longing eyes may hope at

laft their only wifh to fee.   But how, my De-

lia, will you meet The man you've loft fo long ?

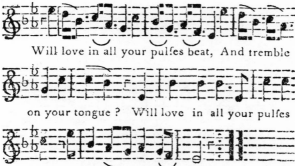

Will love in all your pulſes beat, And tremble

on your tongue ? Will love in all your pulſes

beat, And tremble on yonr tongue ?

Will you in ev'ry look declare
    Your heart is ſtill the ſame ?
And heal each idly anxious care,
    Our fears in abſcence frame ?
Thus, Delia, thus I paint the ſcene,
    When we ſhall ſhortly meet ;
And try what yet remains between,
    Of loit'ring time to cheat !

But if the dream that ſoothes my mind,
    Shall falſe and groundleſs prove ;
If I am doom'd at length to find
    You have forgot to love :
All I of Venus aſk is this,
    No more to let us join ;
But grant me here the flatt'ring bliſs,
    To die and think you mine.

SONG XII.

COME NOW ALL YE SOCIAL POW'RS.

Come now all ye focial pow'rs Shed your in-

fluence o'er us, Crown with joy the prefent hours,

En-li-ven thofe before us. Bring the flafk, the

mufic bring, joy fhall quickly find us, Drink

and dance, and laugh and fing, And caft dull

Chorus.

care behind us.   Bring the flafk, the mufic

bring, Joy shall quickly find us, Drink and dance,

and laugh and sing, And cast dull care behind us.

> Friendship, with thy pow'r divine,
>   Brighten all our features ;
> What but friendship, love, and wine,
>   Can make us happy creatures ?
>   Bring the flask, &c.
>
> Love, thy Godhead we adore,
>   Source of generous passion ;
> Nor will we ever bow before
>   Those idols, wealth and fashion.
>   Bring the flask, &c.
>
> Why should we be dull or sad,
>   Since on earth we moulder ?
> The grave, the gay, the good, the bad,
>   They every day grow older.
>   Bring the flask, &c.
>
> Then since time will steal away,
>   'Spite of all our sorrow ;
> Heighten every joy to day,
>   And never mind to morrow.
>   Bring the flask, &c.

SONG XIII.

BATCHELORS HALL.

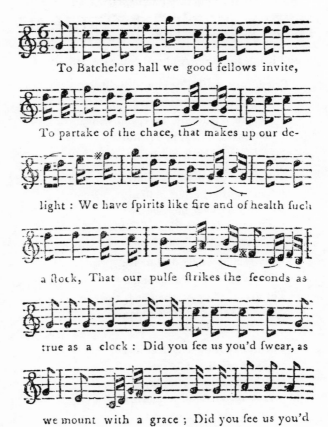

To Batchelors hall we good fellows invite,

To partake of the chace, that makes up our de-

light : We have spirits like fire and of health such

a flock, That our pulse strikes the seconds as

true as a clock : Did you see us you'd swear, as

we mount with a grace ; Did you see us you'd

fwear, As we mount with a grace, That Di-a-na

had dubb'd fome new gods of the chace, That

Di-a-na had dubb'd fome new gods of the chace.

Hark a - way, hark away, All nature looks gay,

And Aurora with fmiles ufh-ers in the bright day.

Dick Thickfet came mounted upon a fine black,
A better fleet gelding ne'er hunter did back :
Tom Trig rode a bay, full of mettle and bone,
And gayly Bob Buxon rode proud on a roan ;
But the horfe of all horfes that rivall'd the day,
Was the Squire's Neck-or-nothing, and that was a
    grey.
    Hark away, hark away,
    While our fpirits are gay,
    Let us drink to the joys of the next coming day.

Then for hounds there was Nimble, so well that
    climbs rocks,
And Cocknose, a good one at scenting a Fox,
Little Plunge, like a mole, who with ferret and
    search,
And beetle-brow'd Hawks-eye, so dead at a lurch :
Young Sly-looks, that scents the strong breeze from
    the South,
And musical Echo-well, with his deep mouth.
    Hark away, &c.

Our horses, thus all of the very best blood,
'Tis not likely you'll easily find such a stud ;
And for hounds our opinions with thousands we'll
    back,   (pack :
That all England throughout can't produce such a
Thus having described you dogs, horses, and crew,
Away we set off, for the Fox is in view.
    Hark away, &c.

Sly Reynard's brought home, while the horns sound
    a call,
And now you're all welcome to Batchelor's hall
The savory sir-loin grateful smokes on the board,
And Bacchus pours wine from his favorite hoard ;
Come on then, do honour to this jovial place.
And enjoy the sweet pleasures that spring from the
    Hark away, &c.   (chace.

SONG XIV.

WOOLF's ADIEU.

Too soon my dearest Sophia, pray take this

kind a - dieu, Oh! love thy pains how bit - ter,

thy joys how short, how few; No more those eyes so

kill - ing, that gentle glance re - peat, Nor

bosom   gently   swelling, with love's soft tumults beat.

Two passions strongly pleading, my doleful heart divide,
Lo ! there's my country bleeding, and here's my weeping bride,
But know thy faithful lover, can true to either prove,
War fires my veins all over, whilst every pulse beats love.

I go where glory leads me, or points the dangerous way,
Tho' coward love upbraids me, yet honour bids obey,
But honours boasting stories, too oft thy swain reprove,
And whisper fame with glory, ah ! what is that to love.

Then think where e'er I wander, through parts by sea or land,
No distant heart can sunder, what mutual love has join'd,
Kind heav'n the brave requiting, shall safe thy swain restore,
And raptures crown the meeting, as love ne'er felt before.

SONG XV.

MARLBOROUGH'S GHOST.

Awful   Hero,   Marlb'ro' rise !

Sleepy charms I come to break ; Hither turn thy

languid eyes, Lo, thy genius calls, awake !

Well survey this faithful plan, Which records thy

life's great name, 'Tis a fhort but crowded fpan,

Full of triumph,   full of fame.

One by one thy deeds review,
  Sieges, battles, thick appear,
Former wonders, loft in new,
  Greatly fill each rifing year.

This is Blenheim's crimfon field,
  Wet with gore, with flaughter ftain'd,
Here retiring fquadrons yield,
  And a bloodlefs wreath is gain'd.

Ponder in thy godlike mind,
   All the wonders thou haft wrought,
Tyrants from their pride declin'd,
   Be the fubject of thy thought.

Reft thee here, while life may laft,
   Th' utmoft blifs to man allow'd
Is to trace his actions paft,
   And to find them great and good.

But 'tis gone ! oh mortal born,
   Swift the fading fcene remove,
Let them pafs with noble fcorn,
   Thine are worlds which roll above.

Poets, prophets, heroes, kings,
   Pleas'd thy ripe approach forefee,
Men who acted wond'rous things,
   Though they yield in fame to thee.

Foremoft in the patriot band,
   Shining with diftinguifh'd day,
See thy friend Godolphin ftand,
   See he beckons thee away.

Yonder feats and fields of light,
   Let thy ravifh'd thoughts explore,
Wifhing, panting for thy fight,
   Half an angel, man no more.
        D

SONG XVI.

HE STOLE MY TENDER HEART AWAY.

The fields were green, the hills were gay, And

birds were finging on each fpray, When Colin

met me   in   the   grove,   And told me tender

tales of love. Was ever fwain fo blithe as he?

So kind, fo faithful and fo free? In   fpite of

all my friends could fay, Young Colin ftole my

heart away.   In fpite of all my friends could

fay,   Young Colin ftole my heart away.

Whene'er he trips the meads along,
He fweetly joins the woodlark's fong
And when he dances on the green,
There's none fo blithe as Colin feen.
If he's but by I nothing fear ;
For I alone am all his care :
Then, fpite of all my friends can fay,
He's ftole my tender heart away.

My mother chides whene'er I roam,
And feems furpris'd I quit my home
But fhe'd not wonder that I rove,
Did fhe but feel how much I love,
Full well I know the gen'rous fwain
Will never give my bofom pain :
Then, fpite of all my friends can fay,
He's ftole my tender heart away.

SONG XVII.

THE STORM.

Ceafe, Rude Boreas, bluft'ring railer, Lift ye

landfmen all to me, Meffmates, hear a brother

failor fing the dangers of the fea, From bound-

ing billows firft in motion, When the diftant

whirlwinds rife, To the tempeft-troubled ocean,

where the feas contend with fkies,

Lively.

Hark ! the boatfwain hoarfely bawling,—
  By topfail fheets, and haulyards ftand !
Down top-gallants quick be hauling !
  Down your ftay-fails, hand, boys, hand !
Now it frefhens, fet the braces ;
  Quick the top-fail fheets let go ;
Luff, boys, luff, don't make wry faces !
  Up your top-fails nimbly clew.

Slow.

Now all you on down-beds fporting,
  Fondly lock'd in beauty's arms,
Frefh enjoyments wanton courting,
  Free from all but love's alarms—
Round us roars the tempeft louder ;
  Think what fear our mind enthrals
Harder yet, it yet blows harder ;
  Now again the boatfwain calls,

Quick.

The top-fail yards point to the wind, boys,
  See all clear to reef each courfe !
Let the forefheets go ; don't mind, boys,
  Though the weather fhould be worfe,
Fore and aft the fprit-fail yard get ;
  Reef the mizen ; fee all clear :
Hand up ! each preventer-brace fet ;
  Man the fore yard ; cheer, lads, cheer !
     D 2

Slow.

Now the dreadful thunder's roaring !
  Peals on peals contending clash !
On our heads fierce rain falls pouring !
  In our eyes blue lightnings flash !
One wide water all around us,
  All above us one black sky !
Diff'rent deaths at once surround us,
  Hark ! what means that dreadful cry ?

Quick.

The foremast's gone, cries ev'ry tongue out,
  O'er the lee, 'twelve feet 'bove deck.
A leak beneath the chest tree's sprung out ;
  Call all hands to clear the wreck.
Quick the lanyards cut to pieces !
  Come, my hearts, be stout and bold !
Plumb the well, the leak increases,
  Four feet water in the hold.

Slow.

While o'er the ship wild waves are beating,
  We for wives or children mourn ;
Alas ! from hence there's no retreating ;
  Alas ! from hence there's no return.
Still the leak is gaining on us,
  Both chain-pumps are chok'd below,
Heav'n have mercy here upon us !
  For only that can save us now !

Quick.

O'er the lee-beam is the land, boys;
　Let the guns o'erboard be thrown;
To the pump come every hand, boys;
　See our mizen-maſt is gone,
The leak we've found, it cannot pour faſt :
　We've lighten'd her a foot or more;
Up, and rig a jury fore-maſt;
　She rights, ſhe rights, boys! wear off ſhore.

Now once more on joys we're thinking,
　Since kind fortune ſpar'd our lives;
Come, the cann, boys, let's be drinking
　To our ſweethearts and our wives.
Fill it up, about ſhip wheel it;
　Cloſe to th' lips a brimmer join.
Where's the tempeſt now? who feels it?
　None! our danger's drown'd in wine!

SONG XVIII.

NOTHING LIKE GROG.

A plague of thoſe muſty old lubbers, Who

tell us to faft and to think, And patient fall in

with life's rubbers, With nothing but water to

drink : A cann of good ftuff had they twigg'd

it, Would have fet them for pleafure a - - gog.

And fpite of the rules, And fpite of the rules

of the fchools, The old fools would have all

of 'em fwigg'd it, And fwore there was

nothing like grog.

My father, when laſt I from Guinea
   Return'd with abundance of wealth,
Cried---Jack, never be ſuch a ninny
   To drink---Says I—father, your health.
So I paſs'd round the ſtuff—ſoon he twigg'd it,
   And it ſet the old codger agog,
     And he ſwigg'd, and mother,
     And ſiſter and brother,
And I ſwigg'd, and all of us ſwigg'd it,
   And ſwore there was nothing like grog.

One day, when the Chaplain was preaching,
   Behind him I curiouſly ſunk,
And, while he our duty was teaching,
   As how we ſhould never get drunk,
I tipt him the ſtuff, and he twigg'd it,
   Which ſoon ſet his rev'rence agog.
     And he ſwigg'd, and Nick ſwigg'd,
     And Ben ſwigg'd, and Dick ſwigg'd,
And I ſwigg'd, and all of us ſwigg'd it,
   And ſwore there was nothing like grog.

Then truſt me there's nothing as drinking
   So pleaſant on this ſide the grave ;
It keeps the unhappy from thinking,
   And makes e'en more valiant the brave.
For, me, from the moment I twigg'd it,
   The good ſtuff has ſo ſet me agog,

Sick or well, late or early,
   Wind foully or fairly,
   I've conftantly fwigg'd it,
And dam'me there's nothing like grog.

SONG XIX.

POOR JACK.

Go patter to lubbers and fwabs, do ye fee,

'Bout danger and fear and the like, A tight

water boat and good fea-room give me. And

t'ent to a little I'll ftrike. Tho' the tempeft top-

gallant mafts fmack fmooth fhould fmite, And

fhiver each fplinter of wood, And fhiver each

splinter of wood. Clear the wreck, stow

the yards, and bouze ev'ry thing tight, And

under reef'd forefail we'll fcud :—Avaft, nor

don't think me a milk-fop fo foft, To be taken

for trifles a - - back. For they fay there's a

providence fits up a loft, They fay there's a pro-

vidence fits aloft, to keep watch for the life

of Poor Jack.

Why I heard the good chaplain palaver one day
   About fouls, heaven, mercy, and fuch,
And, my timbers, what lingo he'd coil and belay,
   Why 'twas juft all as one as high Dutch ;
But he faid how a fparrow can't founder, d'ye fee,
   Without orders that comes down below,
And many fine things that prov'd clearly to me,
   That Providence takes us in tow ;
For fays he, do you mind me, let ftorms e'er fo oft
   Take the top fail of failors aback,
There's a fweet little cherub that fits up aloft
   To keep watch for the life of Poor Jack.

I faid to our Poll, for you fee fhe would cry,
   When laft we weighed anchor for fea,
What argufies fniv'ling and piping your eye ?
   Why what a damn'd fool you muft be :
Can't you fee the world's wide and there's room for
     us all,
   Both for feamen and lubbers afhore ;
And if to old Davy I fhould go, friend Poll,
   Why you never will hear of me more :
What then, all's a hazard, come don't be fo foft,
   Perhaps I may laughing come back,
  or d'ye fee there's a cherub fits fmiling aloft,
   To keep watch for the life of Poor Jack.

Ɔ ye mind me, a failor fhould be every inch
　　All as one as a piece of a fhip,
And with her brave the world, without offering to
　　　flinch,
　　From the moment the anchor's a trip :
As for me, in all weathers, all times, fides, and ends,
　　Nought's a trouble from duty that fprings,
For my heart is my Poll's, and my rhino my friend's,
　　And as for my life 'tis the king's.
Even when my time comes ne'er believe me fo foft,
　　As with grief to be taken aback :
That fame little cherub that fits up aloft,
　　Will look out a good birth for Poor Jack.

SONG XX.

THE SPINNING WHEEL.

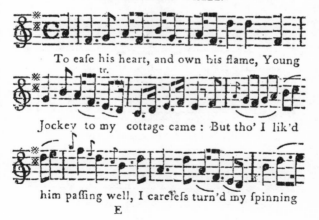

To eafe his heart, and own his flame, Young

Jockey to my cottage came : But tho' I lik'd

him paffing well, I careléfs turn'd my fpinning

E

wheel. My milk-white hand he did extol, And

prais'd my fingers long and small,   Unusual

joy my heart did feel, But still I turn'd my

spinning wheel. Then round about my slender

waist He clasp'd his arms, and me embrac'd,

To kifs my hand he down did kneel, But yet

I turn'd my fpin-ning wheel. With gentle voice

I bid him rife ; He blefs'd my neck, my lips

and eyes ; My fondnefs I could fcarce conceal,

Yet ftill I turn'd my fpinning wheel.   Till

bolder grown, fo clofe he prefs'd, His wanton

thoughts I quickly guefs'd, Then pufh'd him

from my   rock and reel, And angry turn'd

my fpin-ning wheel.   At laft, when I be-

gan to chide, He fwore he meant me for his

bride : 'Twas then my love I did re---veal,

And flung a-way my fpinning wheel.

SONG XXI.

THE GRASSHOPPER.

Little infect that on high, On a fpire

of fpringing grafs, Tipfy with the morning

dew, Free from care thy life doth pa - - - - fs.

Free from care thy life doth pafs.

Sym.

So may'ft thou companion fole,
　Pleafe the lonely mower's ear,
And no treach'rous winding fnake,
　Glide beneath, to work thee fear.

As in chirping plaintive notes
　Thou the hafty fun doft chide,
And with murm'ring mufic charm,
　Summer charming to abide.

E 2

If a pleafant day arrive,
 Soon a pleafant day is gone ;
While we reach to feize our joys
 Swift the winged blifs is flown,

Pain and forrow dwell with us,
 Pleafure fcarce a moment reigns ;
Thou thyfelf find'ft fummer fhort,
 But the winter long remains.

SONG XXII.

THE GALLEY SLAVE.

Oh think on my fate once I freedom enjoy'd,

Was as happy as happy could be, But

pleafure is fled, even hope is deftroy'd !

A captive, alas, on the fea : I was ta'en

by the foe, 'twas the fiat of fate, To

tear me from her I adore. When tho't brings to

mind my once happy eftate, I figh, I

figh as I tug at the oar.

Hard, hard is my fate, oh ! how galling my chain,
  My life's fteer'd by mifery's chart,
And though 'gainft my tyrants I fcorn to complain,
  Tears gufh forth to eafe my fad heart ;
I difdain e'en to fhrink, tho' I feel fharp the lafh,
  Yet my breaft bleeds for her I adore.
While around me the unfeeling billows will dafh,
  I figh and ftill tug at the oar.

How fortune deceives ! I had pleafure in tow,
  The port where fhe dwelt we'd in view ;

But the wifh'd nuptial morn was o'erclouded with
    woe,
  And, dear Anne, I hurried from you.
Our fhallop was boarded and I borne away,
  To behold my dear Anne no more ;
But defpair waftes my fpirits, my form feels decay.
  He figh'd, and expir'd at the oar !

SONG XXIII.

SHEEP IN THE CLUSTERS.

Her fheep had in clufters crept clofe by the

grove, To hide from the rigors of day ; And

Phillis herfelf in a woodbine alcove, A-

mong the green vi - o - lets lay.

Among the green violets lay.

A youngling it feems had been ftole from its dam—
  'Twixt Cupid and Hymen a plot—
That Corydon might, as he fearch'd for his lamb,
  Arrive at this critical fpot.

As thro' the gay hedge for his lambkin he peeps,
  He faw the fweet maid with furprife :
Ye Gods ! if fo killing, he cri'd, when fhe fleeps,
  I'm loft if fhe opens her eyes.

To tarry much longer would hazard my heart,
  I'll onward my lambkin to trace ;
In vain honeft Corydon ftrove to depart,
  For love had him nail'd to the place.

Hufh, hufh be thofe birds, what a bawling they keep ;
  He cri'd, you're too loud on the fpray ;—
Don't you fee, foolifh lark, that my charmer's afleep,
  You'll wake her as fure as 'tis day.

How dares that fond butterfly touch the fweet maid,
  Her cheek he miftakes for the rofe ;
I'd pat him to death if I were not afraid
  That my boldnefs would break her repofe.

Young Phillis look 'd up with a languifhing fmile,
  Kind fhepherd, fhe faid, you miftake ;
I laid myfelf down juft to reft me awhile,
  But, truft me, have ftill been awake.

The fhepherd took courage, advanc'd with a bow,
　　And plac'd himfelf clofe by her fide,
And manag'd the matter I cannot tell how,
　　But yefterday made her his bride.

SONG XXIV.

WHEN BIDDEN TO THE WAKE.

When bidden to the wake or fair, The

joy of each free hearted fwain, Till Phebe

promis'd to be there, I loiter'd laft of

all the train. If chance fome fairing caught her

eye, The ribbon gay, or filken glove,

With eager hafte I ran to buy, For what

is gold compar'd to love.

My pofy on her bofom plac'd
Could Harry's fweeter fcents exhale,
Her auburn locks my ribbon grac'd,
And flutter'd in the wanton gale ;
With fcorn fhe hears me now complain,
Nor can my ruftic prefents move ;
Her heart prefers a richer fwain,
And gold, alas ! has banifh'd love.

SONG XXV.

ALONE BY THE LIGHT OF THE MOON.

The day is departed, and round from the

cloud The moon in her beauty appears ; The

voice of the nightingale warbles aloud The

muſic of love in our ears, Maria appear !

now the ſeaſon ſo ſweet With the beat of the

heart is in tune ; The time is ſo tender for

lovers to meet Alone by the light of the

moon, Alone by the light of the moon, Alone

by the light of the moon, A-lone by the light

of the moon, A - - - lone by the light of

the moon.

I cannot when prefent unfold what I feel ;
   I figh---Can a lover do more ?
Her name to the fhepherds I never reveal,
   Yet I think of her all the day o'er.
Maria, my love ! do you long for the grove,
   Do you figh for an interview foon ;
Does e'er a kind thought run on me as you rove,
   Alone by the light of the Moon ?

Your name from the fhepherds, whenever I hear,
   My bofom is all in a glow ;
Your voice, when it vibrates, fo fweet thro' mine ear,
   My heart thrills---my eyes overflow.
Ye pow'rs of the fky, will your bounty divine
   Indulge a fond lover his boon ;
Shall heart fpring to heart, and Maria be mine
   Alone by the light of the Moon ?

F

SONG XXVI.

AH WHY MUST WORDS.

Ah why muft words my flame reveal ? What

needs my Damon bid me tell What all my ac-

tions prove ? What all my actions prove.

A blufh whene'er I meet his eye, When-

e'er I hear his name A figh betrays my fe-

cret love,   betrays my fecret love.

In all their fports upon the plain
My eyes ftill fix'd on him remain,
　　And him alone approve ;
The reft unheeded, dance or play,
He fteals from all my praife away,
　　And can he doubt my love ?

Whene'er we meet, my looks confefs
The pleafures which my foul poffefs,
　　And all its cares remove.
Still, ftill too fhort appears his ftay,
I frame excufes for delay,
　　Can this be ought but love ?

Does any fpeak in Damon's praife,
How pleas'd am I with all he fays,
　　And every word approve ;
Is he defamed, tho' but in jeft,
I feel refentment fire my breaft,
　　Alas ! becaufe I love.

But O ! what tortures tear my heart,
When I fufpect his looks impart
　　The leaft defire to rove.
I hate the maid who gives me pain,
Yet him I ftrive to hate in vain,
　　For ah ! that hate is love.

Then afk not words, but read my eyes,

Believe my blufhes, truft my fighs,

    All thefe my paffion prove :

Words may deceive, may fpring from art,

But the true language of my heart

    To Damon muft be love.

SONG XXVII.

WHEN FIRST I SLIPP'D MY LEADING STRINGS.

When firft I flipp'd my leading ftrings, To pleafe

her little   Poll,   My mother bought me at the

fair, A   pretty   waxen Doll ;   Such   floe

black eyes and cherry cheeks The fmiling dear pof-

fefs'd, How could I kifs it   oft enough, Or hug

it to my breaſt, How could I kiſs it oft enough,

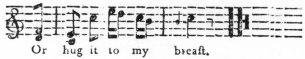

Or hug it to my breaſt.

Nó ſooner I could chatter too,
　As moſt young Miſſes do,
Than how I long'd and ſigh'd to hear,
　My Dolly prattle too ;
I curl'd her hair in ringlets neat,
　And dreſt her very gay,
But yet the ſulky huſſy not
　A ſyllable would ſay.

Provok'd that to my queſtions kind,
　No anſwer I could get,
I ſhook the little huſſy well,
　And whip'd her in a pet,
My mother cri'd, O fie upon't,
　Pray let your Doll alone,
If e'er you wiſh and hope to ſee
　A baby of your own.

My head on this I bridled up,
　And threw the plaything by,
F 2

Altho' my fifter fnub'd me for it,
  I know the reafon why;
I fancy fhe would wifh to keep,
  The fweethearts all her own,
But that fhe fhan't depend upon't,
  When I'm a woman grown.

SONG XXVIII.

NANCY, or, THE SAILOR's JOURNAL.

'Twas paft me - - ri - - dian half paft

four, By fignal I from Nancy parted;

At fix fhe lin - ger'd on the fhore,

With uplift hands, and broken hearted: At fev'n,

while taughtening the foreſtay, I ſaw her

faint, or elſe 'twas fancy ; At eight we

all got under way, And bid a

long adieu to Nancy.

Night came, and now eight bells had rung,
While careleſs Sailors, ever cheary,
　On the mid watch ſo jovial ſung,
With tempers labour cannot weary.
　I little to their mirth inclin'd,
While tender thoughts ruſh'd on my fancy,
　And my warm ſighs increas'd the wind,
Look'd on the moon, and thought of Nancy.

　And now arrived that jovial night,
When every true bred tar carouſes,
　When, o'er the grog all hands delight
To toaſt their ſweethearts and their ſpouſes.

Round went the can, the jeſt, the glee,
While tender wiſhes fill'd each fancy ;
  And when, in turn, it came to me,
I heav'd a ſigh, and toaſted Nancy.

Next morn a ſtorm came on at four,
At ſix, the elements in motion;
  Plunged me and three poor Sailors more
Headlong within the foaming ocean.
  Poor wretches ! they ſoon found their graves—
For me, it may be only fancy,
  But Love ſeemed to forbid the waves
To ſnatch me from the arms of Nancy.

Scarce the foul hurricane was cleared,
Scarce winds and waves had ceaſed to rattle,
  When a bold enemy appeared,
And, dauntleſs, we prepared for battle.
  And now, while ſome loved friend or wife,
Like light'ning, ruſhed on every fancy,
  To Providence I truſted life,
Put up a prayer, and thought on Nancy.

At laſt, 'twas in the month of May,
The crew, it being lovely weather,
  At three, A. M. diſcovered day,
And England's chalky cliffs together.
  At ſeven, up channel how we bore,
While hopes and fears ruſhed on my fancy,
  At twelve I gaily jumped aſhore.
And to my throbbing heart preſſed Nancy.

SONG XXIX.

STERNE's MARIA.

'Twas near a thickets calm retreat, Be-

neath a poplar tree, Ma - ri - a chofe

her wretched feat, To mourn her forrows

free; Her lovely form was fweet to

view, As dawn at opening day ; But

ah, fhe mourn'd her love not true, And wept

her cares a - way.

The brook flow'd gently at her feet,
    In murmurs smooth along;
Her pipe which once she tun'd most sweet,
    Has now forgot its song;
No more to charm the vale she tries,
    For grief has fill'd her breast;
Those joys that once she used to prize,
    Ere love destroy'd her rest.

Poor hapless maid! Who can behold
    Thy sorrows so severe?
And hear thy lovelorn story told,
    Without a falling tear.
Maria! luckless maid, adieu,
    Thy sorrows soon must cease;
For Heav'n will take a maid so true,
    To everlasting peace.

SONG XXX.

I SOLD A GUILTLESS NEGRO BOY.

When thirst of gold enslaves the mind, And

selfish views a - lone bear sway, And self-

ish   views a-lone bear ſway, Man turns a

ſavage   to his kind, And blood, and ra - pine

mark his way, And blood and   ra - pine mark

his way,   A - - las,   for   this   poor

ſimple toy   I   ſold   a   guiltleſs Negro

Boy,   I ſold a guiltleſs · Negro Boy.

His father's hope, his mother's pride,
Tho' black yet comely to the view,
I tore him helpleſs from their ſide,
And gave him to a ruffian crew.
Alas, for this poor ſimple toy
I ſold a guiltleſs Negro Boy.

In ifles that deck the weftern main,
  Th' unhappy youth was doom'd to dwell,
A poor forlorn infulted flave,
  A beaft that Chriftians buy and fell.
    To fiends, that Afric's coaft annoy
    I fold a guiltlefs Negro Boy.

May he who walks upon the wind,
  Whofe voice in thunder's heard on high,
Who doft the raging tempeft bind,
  And wings the lightning thro' the fky,
    Forgive the wretch that for a toy
    Could fell a helplefs Negro Boy.

SONG XXXI.

THE HOBBIES.

Attention pray give, while of hobbies I fing,

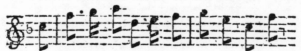

For each has his hobby from cobbler to king;

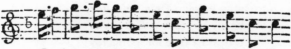

On fome fav'rite hobby we all get aftride,

And when we're once mounted full gallop we ride.

All on hob - bies,   All on hob bies,

All   on hobbies, Gee up, gee O !

Some hobbies are reſtive, and hard for to govern,
E'en juſt like our wives, they're ſo curſedly ſtubborn :
The hobbies of ſcolds, are their huſbands to teaze,
And the hobbies of lawyers, are plenty of fees.

    That's their hobby, &c.

The beaux, thoſe ſweet gentlemen's hobbies good lack,
Is to wear great large poultices tied round the neck ;
And think in the ton and the tippy they're dreſt,
If they've b reeches that reach from the ancle to cheſt.

    That's their hobby, &c.

The hobbies of ſailors, when ſafe moor'd in port,
Are their wives and their ſweethearts to toy with,
    and ſport :
When our navy's completed, their hobby ſhall be,
To ſhow the whole world that America's Free.

    That's their hobby, &c.

        G

The hobbies of foldiers, in time of great wars,
Are breaches and battles, with blood, wounds and fcars;
But in peace, you'll obferve that quite diff'rent their
　　　trade is,
The hobbies of foldiers in peace, are the ladies.
　　　That's their hobby, &c.

The ladies fweet creatures, yes, they now and then,
Get aftride of their hobbies, e'en juft like the men;
With fmiles and with fimpers beguile us with eafe,
And we gallop, trot, amble e'en juft as they pleafe.
　　　That's their hobby, &c.

The American's hobby has long fince been known,
No tyrant or king fhall from them have a throne ;
Their States are united and let it be faid,
Their hobby is WASHINGTON, Peace and Free Trade.
　　　That's their hobby, &c.

SONG XXXII.

AH DELIA SEE THE FATAL HOUR.

Ah Delia fee the　fa-tal hour, Farewell my foul's de　light;　But how fhall

wretched Damon live, Thus banifh'd from thy

fight,   To   my fond heart no   ri - val

joy Supplies the lofs of   thee ;   But   who

can tell,   if   thou my dear Will   e'er re-

member   me.   D. C.

Yet while my reftlefs wand ring thoughts,
　　Purfue their loft repofe ;
Unweary'd may they trace the path,
　　Where'er my Delia goes :
Forever Damon fhall be there
　　Attendant on the way.
　　　　But who can tell, &c.

Alone through unfrequented wilds,
　　With penfive fteps I rove,
I afk the rocks, I afk the ftreams,
　　Where dwells my diftant Love :
The filent eve the rofy morn
　　My conftant fearch furvey,
　　　But who can tell, &c.

Oft I'll review the fmiling fcene,
　　Each fav'rite brook and tree ;
Where gaily pafs'd the happy hours,
　　Thofe hours I pafs'd with thee ;
What painful fond memorials rife
　　From ev'ry place I fee.
　　　Ah, who can tell, &c.

How many rival votaries foon,
　　Their foft addrefs fhall move ;
Surround thee in thy new abode,
　　And tempt thy foul to Love :
Ah, who can tell when fighing crowds,
　　Their tender homage pay,
　　　Ah, who can tell, &c.

Think, Delia, with how deep a wound
　　The fweetly painful dart,
Which thy remembrance leaves behind,
　　Has pierc'd a hopelefs heart :
Think on this fatal, fad adieu,
　　That fevers me from thee.
　　　Ah, who can tell, &c.

SONG XXXIII.

GOLDEN DAYS OF GOOD QUEEN BESS.

To my mufe give attention, and deem it

not a myftery, If we jumble together mufic,

poetry, and hiftory : The times to difplay in

the days of Queen Befs, fir, Whofe name and

whofe mem'ry po-fte-ri-ty may blefs, fir. O the

golden days of good Queen Befs ; Merry be the

memory of good Queen Befs.

Then we laugh'd at the bugbears of dons and armadas,
With their gunpowder puffs, and their bluftering
    bravadoes ;
For we knew how to manage both the mufket and
    the bow, fir,
And could bring down a Spaniard juft as eafy as a
    crow, fir.
        O the golden days, &c.

Then our ftreets were unpav'd, and our houfes were
    thatch'd, fir,
Our windows were lattic'd and our doors only
    latch'd, fir ;
Yet fo few were the folks that would plunder and
    rob, fir,
That the hangman was ftarving for want of a job, fir.
        O the golden days, &c.

Then our ladies with large ruffs tied round about the
    neck faft,
Would gobble up a pound of beef fteaks for their
    breakfaft ;
While a clofe quil'd-up coif their noddles juft did
    fit, fir,
And they trufs'd up as tight as a rabbit for the fpit,
    fir.
        O the golden days, &c.

Then jerkins, and doublets, and yellow worſted hoſe,
    ſir,
With a huge pair of whiſkers, was the dreſs of our
    beaux, ſir,
Strong beer they preferr'd to claret or to hock, ſir,
And no poultry they priz'd like the wing of an ox, ſir.
        O the golden days, &c.

Good neighbourhood then was as plenty too as beef,
    ſir,
And the poor from the rich ne'er wanted relief, ſir,
While merry went the mill clack, the ſhuttle and the
    plow, ſir,
And honeſt men could live by the ſweat of their
    brow, ſir.
        O the golden days, &c.

Then football, and wreſtling, and pitching of the bar,
    ſir,
Were preferr'd to a flute, to a fiddle, or guitar, ſir :
And for jaunting, and junketting, the fav'rite regale,
    ſir,
Was a walk as far as Chelſea, to demoliſh buns and
    ale, ſir,
        O the golden days, &c.

Then the folks, ev'ry Sunday, went twice at leaſt to
    church, ſir,
And never left the parſon or his ſermon in the
    lurch, ſir,

For they judg'd that the Sabbath was for people to be
    good in, fir,
And they thought it Sabbath-breaking if they din'd
    without a pudding, fir.
        O the golden days, &c.

Then our great men were good, and our good men
    were great, fir,
And the props of the nation were the pillars of the
    ftate, fir ;
For the fov'reign an fubject one intereft fupported,
And our powerful alliance by all powers then was
    courted.
        O the golden days, &c.

Then the high and mighty ftates, to their everlafting
    ftain, fir,
By Britons were releas'd from the galling yoke of
    Spain, fir,
And the rous'd Britifh lion, had all Europe then
    combin'd, fir,
Undifmay'd would have fcatter'd them, like chaff
    before the wind, fir,
        O the golden days, &c.

Thus they ate, and they drank, and they work'd, and
    they play'd, fir,
Of their friends not afham'd, nor of enemies afraid, fir,

And little did they think, when this ground they
 ſtood on, ſir,
To be drawn from the life, now they're all dead and
 gone, ſir.
          O the golden days, &c.

THE GOLDEN DAYS WE NOW POSSESS.

A Sequel to the favorite Song of Good Queen Beſs.

To the foregoing Tune.

IN the praiſe of Queen Beſs lofty ſtrains have been
 ſung ſir ;
And her fame has been echo'd by old and by young,
 ſr ;
But from times that are paſt we'll for once turn our
 eyes, ſir,
As the times we enjoy 'tis but wiſdom to prize, ſir,
Then whate'er were the days of Good Queen Beſs.
Let us praiſe the golden days we now poſſeſs.

Without armies to combat, or armadas to withſtand
 ſir,
Our foes at our feet, and the ſword in our hand, ſir,
Laſting peace we ſecure while we're Lords of the
 ſeas, ſir,
And our ſtout wooden walls are our ſure guarantees,
 ſir.
     Such are the golden days we now poſſeſs,
     Whatever were the days of Good Queen Beſs.

No Bigots rule the roaſt, now, with perſecution dire,
 ſir,
Burning zeal now no more heaps the faggot on the
 fire, ſir ;

No bifhop now can broil a poor Jew like a pidgeon,
  fir ;
Nor barbacue a Pagan, like a pig, for religion, fir.
    Such are, &c.

Now no legendary faint robs the lab'rer of one day,
Except now and then when he celebrates St. Monday:
And good folks, ev'ry fabbath, keep church without
  a pother, fir,
By walking in at one door, and ftealing out at t'other,
  fir.
    Such are, &c.

Then for drefs—modern belles bear the bell beyond
  compare, fir,
Though farthingales and ruffs are got rather out of
  wear, fir ;
But when trufs'd up, like pullets, whether fat, lean,
  or plump, fir,
'Tis no matter, fo they've got but a merry thought
  and rump, fir,
    Such are, &c.

Such promontories, fure, may be ftil'd inacceffibles,
As our fmall-cloaths, by prudes, are pronounc'd inex-
  preffibles ;
And the tafte of our beaux won't admit of difpute, fir,
When they ride in their flippers, and walk about in
  boots, fir,
    Such are, &c.

Our language is refin'd too, from what 'twas of yore,
  fir,
As a flice ftring's the dandy, and a buckle's quite a
  bore, fir ;
And if rais'd from the dead, it would fure poze the
  noddle, fir,
Of a Snakfpeare, to tell what's the Tippy, or the
  Twaddle, fir,
    Such are, &c.

Then for props of the ftate, what can equal in ftory,
  fir,
Thofe two ftately pillars, call'd a Whig and a Tory,
  fir ;
Though by fhifting their ground, they fometimes get
  fo wrong, fir,
They forget to which fide of the houfe they belong,
  fir.
    Such are, &c.

But as props of their ftrength and uprightnefs may
  boaft, fir,
While the proudeft of pillars may be fhook by a poft
  fir ;
May the firm friends of freedom her bleffings inherit,
  fir,
And her foes be advanc'd to the the poft which they
  merit, fir.
    Then fhall the golden days we now poffefs
    Far furpafs the boafted days of good Queen Befs.

And as the name of Brunfwick claims duty, love,
  and awe, fir,
Far beyond a Plantagenet, a Tudor, or Naffau, fir,
Let the fceptre be fway'd by the fon or the fire, fir,
May their race rule this land till the globe is on fire,
  fir ;
    And may their future days, in glory and fuccefs,
    .Far furpafs the golden days we now poffefs.

SONG XXXIV.

BRIGHT PHŒBUS.

Bright Phœbus has mounted the chariot of day,

And the horns and the hounds call each sportf-

man a-way ; And the horns and the hounds call

each sportfman away. Thro' woods and thro'

meadows with fpeed now they bound, While

health, ro-ly health, is in ex-er-cife found ;

Thro' woods and thro' meadows with fpeed now

they bound, While health, rosy health, is in

ex-er-cise found.   Hark away!   Hark a-

way!   Hark away is the word to the sound

of the horn -

- - - - - - - - - - - - - - - - And e - cho   and

e - - cho,   And e - - cho, blithe e - cho, makes

jo- vial the morn.
H

Each hill and each valley is lovely to view,
While pufs flies the covert, and dogs quick purfue.
Behold where fhe flies o'er the wide-fpreading plain !
While the loud op'ning pack purfue her amain.

 Hark away, &c.

At length pufs is caught, and lies panting for breath,
And the fhout of the huntfman's the fignal for death,
No joys can delight like the fports of the field ;
To hunting all pleafurs and paftimes muft yield.

 Hark away, &c.

SONG XXXV.

THE ROSARY.

Tho' oft we meet fevere diftrefs In ven'ring out to fea, Tho' oft we meet fevere diftrefs in vent'ring out to fea, The perils of the ftorm feems lefs, As we to heav'n our

vows addrefs, And fing the cheering   Rofary,

I fing the cheering Ro-fa-ry, As we to

heav'n our vows addrefs, I fing the cheering

Ro - fa - ry.   *173101*

Our kids, that rove the mountain wide,
    And bound in harmlefs glee,
I feek each day at eventide,
And while their courfe I homeward guide,
    I fing the cheering Rofary.

And in the deeper fhades of night,
While thro' the woods I flee,
Where gloom and filence yield afright,
To make my beating heart fit light,
    I fing the cheering Rofary.

SONG XXXVI.

DIOGENES SURLY AND PROUD.

Di-o-ge-nes furly and proud, Who fnarl'd at

the Macedon youth, Delighted in wine that was

good, Becaufe in good wine there is truth ; But

growing as poor as a Job, And un-a-ble to pur-

chafe a flafk. He chofe for his manfion a tub,

And liv'd by the fcent of his ca - - - - - - - - - -

- - - - - - - - - - - fk, And liv'd by the fcent

of his cafk.

Heraclitus would never deny
 A bumper to cherish his heart ;
And, when he was maudlin, would cry ;
 Because he had empty'd his quart :
Though some were so foolish to think
 He wept at men's folly and vice,
When 'twas only his custom to drink
 'Till the liquor ran out at his eyes.

Democritus alway was glad
 To tipple and cherish his soul ;
Would laugh like a man that was mad,
 When over a jolly full bowl :
While his cellar with wine was well stor'd,
 His liquor he'd merrily quaff ;
And, when he was drunk as a lord,
 At those that were sober he'd laugh.

Copernicus, too, like the rest,
 Believ'd there was wisdom in wine :
And knew that a cup of the best,
 Made reason the brighter to shine :
With wine he replenish'd his veins,
 And made his philosophy reel :
Then fancy'd the world, as his brains,
 Turn'd round like a chariot wheel.

Aristotle, that master of arts,
 Had been but a dunce without wine ;
    H

For what we afcribe to his parts,
    Is due to the juice of the vine ;
His belly, fome authors agree,
    Was as big as a watering-trough :
He therefore leap'd into the fea,
    Becaufe he'd have liquor enough.

When Pyrrho had taken a glafs,
    He faw that no objeft appear'd
Exaftly the fame as it was
    Before he had liquor'd his beard ;
For things running round in his drink,
    Which fober he motionlefs found,
Occafion'd the fceptic to think
    There was nothing of truth to be found.

Old Plato was reckon'd divine,
    Who wifely to virtue was prone ;
But, had it not been for good wine,
    His merit had never been known :
By wine we are generous made :
    It furnifhes fancy with wings ;
Without it we ne'er fhould have had
    Philofophers, poets, or kings.

SONG XXXVII.

RISE COLUMBIA !

An occasional Song written by Mr. THOMAS PAINE of Boston.

When firſt the Sun o'er O - cean glow'd,

And earth un - - veil'd her virgin breaſt,

Supreme mid Nature's, mid Nature's vaſt abode,

Was heard th'Al - migh - ty's dread beheſt :

Riſe Columbia, Columbia brave and free,

Poize the globe and bound the ſea.

CHORUS.

Rife Columbia,   Columbia brave and free,

Poize the   globe   and bound the fea.

In darknefs wrapp'd, with fetters chain'd ;
   Will ages grope, debas'd and blind,
With blood the human hand be ftain'd—
   With tyrant power, the human mind.
       Rife Columbia, &c.

But, lo ! acrofs th' Atlantic floods,
   The ftar-directed pilgrim fails !
See ! fell'd by Commerce, float thy woods ;
   And cloth'd by Ceres, wave thy vales !
       Rife Columbia, &c.

In vain fhall thrones, in arms combin'd,
  The facred rights I gave, oppofe ;
In thee th' afylum of mankind,
  Shall welcome nations find repofe.
    Rife COLUMBIA, &c.

Nor yet, though fkill'd, delight in arms ;
  PEACE and her offspring ARTS, be thine :
The face of freedom fcarce has charms,
  When, on her cheeks, no dimples fhine.
    Rife COLUMBIA, &c.

While Fame, for thee, her wreath entwines,
  To BLESS, thy nobler triumph prove ;
And though the EAGLE haunts thy PINES,
  Beneath thy WILLOWS fhield the DOVE.
    Rife COLUMBIA, &c.

When bolts the flame, or whelms the wave,
  Be thine, to rule the wayward hour—
Bid DEATH unbar the watery grave,
  And VULCAN yield to NEPTUNE'S pow'r.
    Rife COLUMBIA, &c.

Rever'd in arms, in peace humane—
  No fhore, nor realm fhall bound thy fway,
While all the virtues own thy reign,
  And fubject elements obey !
    Rife COLUMBIA, brave and free,
    Blefs the Globe, and rule the Sea !

SONG XXXVIII.

THE SWEET LITTLE GIRL THAT I LOVE.

My friends all declare that my time is mifpent,

While in rural re - tire-ment I rove, I

afk no more wealth, than dame fortune has fent,

But the fweet little girl that I love; The

fweet lit-tle girl that I love, The rofe on

her cheek's my delight. She's foft as the

down, as the down on the dove, No lilly was

ev-er fo white, As the fweet little girl

that I love.

Tho' humble my cot, calm content gilds the fcene,
    For my fair one delights in my grove,
And a palace I'd quit for a dance on the green,
    With the fweet little girl that I love.

No ambition I know but to call her my own,
    No fame but her praifes to prove,
My happinefs centers in Fanny alone,
    She's the fweet little girl that I love.

SONG XXXIX.

NEW ANACREONTIC SONG.

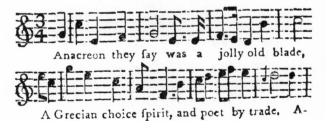

Anacreon they fay was a jolly old blade,

A Grecian choice fpirit, and poet by trade. A-

nacreon, they fay, was a   jolly old blade, A

Grecian choice fpirit, and poet by trade. To

Venus and Bacchus he tun'd up his lays ; For

Love and a bumber he fung all his days : To

Venus and   Bacchus he tun'd up his lays, For

love and a bumper, For love and a   bumper he

fung   all his days.

He laugh'd as he quaff'd ftill the juice of the vine,
And tho' he was human was look'd on divine,
At the feaft of good humour he always was there,
And his fancy and fonnets ftill banifh'd dull care.

Good wine, boys, says he, is the liquor of Jove,
'Tis our comfort below and their nectar above ;
Then while round the table the bumper we pafs,
Let the toaft be to Venus and each fmiling lafs.

Apollo may torment his catgut or wire,
Yet Bacchus and Beauty the theme muft infpire,
Or elfe all his humming and ftrumming is vain,
The true joys of heaven he'd never obtain.

To love and be lov'd how tranfporting the blifs,
While the heart-cheering glafs gives a zeft to each
    kifs ;
With Bacchus and Venus I'll ever combine,
For drinking and kiffing are pleafures divine.

As fons of Anacreon then let us be gay,
With drinking and love pafs the moments away ;
With wine and with beauty let's fill up the fpan,
For that's the beft method, deny it who can.

SONG XL.

THERE WAS A JOLLY MILLER.

There was a jol - ly miller once Liv'd on the

I

ri - ver Dee, He danc'd and he fung from morn

till night, No lark fo blithe as he.   And this the

burden of his fong for e - ver us'd to be :   I

care for nobody, no, not I, If no-bo-dy cares

for me.

I live by my mill, God blefs her ! fhe's kindred, child
    and wife ;
I would not change my ftation for any other in life.
No lawyer, furgeon, or doctor, e'er had a groat from
    me.
I care for nobody, no, not I, if nóbody cares for me.

When fpring begins its merry career, oh ! how his
    heart-grows gay !
No fummer's drought alarms his fears, nor winter's
    fad decay ;

No forefight mars the miller's joy, who's wont to fing
and fay,
Let others toil from year to year, I live from day to
day.

Thus, like the miller, bold and free, let us rejoice and
fing :
The days of youth are made for glee, and time is on
the wing.
This fong fhall pafs from me to thee, along this jovial
ring.
Let heart and voice and all agree, to fay,—long live
the King !

SONG XLI.

THE TWADDLE.

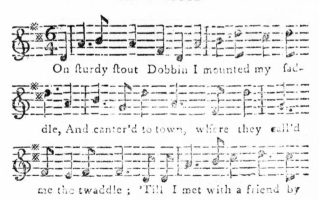

On fturdy ftout Dobbin I mounted my faddle, And canter'd to town, where they call'd
me the twaddle ; 'Till I met with a friend by

mere dint of good luck, Who taught me the

Tippee, And now I'm a buck! To swallow six

bottles I now dare engage, Then to knock down

those watchmen bent double with age, And if

spent with fatigue to St. James's I waddle, To

shew the beau monde I'm no longer the twaddle,

No longer the twaddle, No longer the twaddle,

To shew the beau monde I'm no longer the

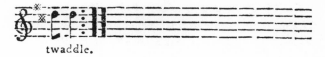

twaddle.

Having now learnt to read why I take in the papers,
And draining a bumper to banifh the vapours,
I fcan the frefh quarrels 'twixt new-married fpoufes,
To match the debates in both Parliament houfes.
Where patriots and placemen keep wrangling for
  fame,
The outs are all faultlefs, the ins are to blame ;
Tho' the outs are the Tippee, their brains are all ad-
  dle,
Yet when they get in you foon find'em the Twaddle.

When Briton's bafe foes dare prefume to unite,
Old Elliot's the Tippee, becaufe he dare fight.
And to poets, who live on the floor next the fky,
Roaft beef is a Tippee they feldom come nigh.
The lawyer and doftor both ftrictly agree
That all is the Twaddle—except 'tis their fee.
And when you from Dover to Calais would ftraddle,
A balloon is the Tippee, a packet's the Twaddle.

Dick Twifting is now quite the Twaddle for tea,
Tho' he once was the Tippee for Green and Bohea ;
But then we'd no tax to turn day into night,
No dire Commutation to block up our light.

"Leaſt ſaid's ſooneſt mended," I hope I'm not wrong,
If I'm pray excuſe, and I'll hence hold my tongue:
Perhaps you may think me a mere fiddle faddle,
Yet if not quite the Tippee, don't ſay I'm the
     Twaddle.

SONG XLII.

THE INDIAN CHIEF.

The ſun ſets at night, and the ſtars ſhun

the day, But Glory re-mains when their lights

fade away: Begin, ye tormentors, your threats

are in vain, For the ſon of Alk-no-mook ſhall

never complain.

Remember the arrows he fhot from his bow,
Remember your chiefs by his hatchet laid low :
Why fo flow?—Do you wait till I fhrink from the
    pain ?
No!—the fon of Alknomook fhall never complain.

Remember the wood where in ambufh we lay,
And the fcalps which we bore from your nation away.
Now the flame rifes faft, they exult in my pain ;
But the fon of Alknomook can never complain.

I go to the land where my father is gone :
His ghoft fhall rejoice in the fame of his fon.
Death comes as a friend, he relieves me from pain :
And the fon of Alknomook has fcorn'd to complain!

SONG XLIII.

HOW HAPPY THE SOLDIER.

How happy the foldier who lives on his pay,

And fpends half a crown out of fixpence a day ;

Yet fears neither juſtices, warrants, or bums,

But pays all his debts with the roll of his drums.

With row de dow, row de dow, row de dow,

dow ; And he pays all his debts with the roll

of his drums.

He cares not a marvedy how the world goes :
His king finds him quarters, and money, and clothes ;
He laughs at all ſorrow whenever it comes,
And rattles away with the roll of his drums.
    With a row de dow, &c.

The drum is his glory, his joy, and delight,
It leads him to pleaſure as well as to fight ;
No girl, when ſhe hears it, tho' ever ſo glum,
But packs up her tatters, and follows the drum.
    With a row de dow, &c.

SONG XLIV.

THE LASSES OF DUBLIN.

The meadows look cheerful, the birds fweet-

ly fing, So gayly they carrol the praifes of

fpring ! Tho' Na-ture rejoices, poor No-rah

fhall mourn, Until her dear Patrick again fhall

return. Tho' gain fhall return.

Ye Laffes of Dublin, ah, hide your gay charms,
Nor lure her dear Patrick from Norah's fond arms;
Tho' fattins, and ribbons, and laces are fine,
They hide not a heart with fuch feeling as mine.

SONG XLV.

ADIEU, ADIEU, MY ONLY LIFE.

A-dieu, adieu, my on-ly life, My honour

calls me from thee : Remember thou'rt a fol-

dier's wife, Thofe tears but ill be - come thee.

What tho' by du - ty I am call'd Where thun-

dering cannons rattle ; Where valour's felf might

ftand appall'd, Where valour's felf might ftand

appall'd ; When on the wings of thy dear love,

To heaven a-bove thy fervent orifons are down ;

The tender pray'r thou put'ft up there, Shall call

a guardian angel down, Shall call a guardian

an - gel down, To watch me in the battle.

My fafety thy fair truth fhall be,
 As fword and buckler ferving,
My life fhall be more dear to me,
 Becaufe of thy preferving.
Let peril come, let horror threat,
 Let thundr'ring cannons rattle,
I fearlefs feek the conflict's heat,
 Affur'd when on the wings of love
  To heaven above, &c.

Enough—with that benignant fmile
 Some kindred God infpir'd thee,
Who faw thy bofom void of guile,
 Who wonder'd and admir'd thee :

I go, aſſur'd—my life! adieu,
Tho' thund'ring cannons rattle,
Tho' murd'ring carnage ſtalk in view,
When on the wings of thy true love,
To heaven above, &c.

SONG XLVI.

SATURDAY NIGHT AT SEA.

'Twas Saturday night, the twinkling ſtars

Shone on the rippling ſea: No duty call'd the

jo - vial tars, The helm was laſh'd a - - lee,

The helm was laſh'd a - - lee. The am - ple

can adorn'd the board, Prepar'd to ſee it

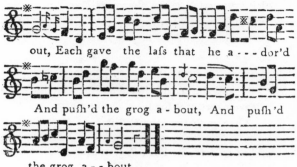

out, Each gave the lafs that he a - - - dor'd

And pufh'd the grog a - bout, And pufh'd

the grog a - - bout.

Cried honeſt Tom, my Peg I'll toaſt,
    A frigate neat and trim,
All jolly Portſmouth's favourite boaſt :
    I'd venture life and limb,
Sail ſeven long years, and ne'er ſee land,
    With dauntleſs heart and ſtout,
So tight a veſſel to command :
    Then puſh the grog about.

I'll give, cried little Jack, my Poll,
    Sailing in comely ſtate,
Top ga'nt-ſails ſet ſhe is ſo tall,
    She looks like a firſt-rate,
Ah ! would ſhe take her Jack in tow,
    A voyage for life throughout,
No better birth I'd wiſh to know :
    Then puſh the grog about,
                K

I'll give, cried I, my charming Nan,
　　Trim, handfome, neat and tight.
What joy, fo neat a fhip to man!
　　Oh ! fhe's my heart's delight.
So well fhe bears the ftorms of life,
　　I'd fail the world throughout,
Brave every toil for fuch a wife ;
　　Then pufh the grog about.

Thus to defcribe Poll, Peg, or Nan,
　　Each his beft manner tried,
Till fummon'd by the empty can,
　　They to their hammocks hied :
Yet ftill did they their vigils keep,
　　Though the huge can was out ;
For in foft vifions gentle fleep
　　Still pufh'd the grog about.

SONG XLVII.

HAIL ! AMERICA HAIL !

Hail ! Amer-i - ca hail ! unrival'd in Fame,

Thy foes in confufion turn pale at thy name ;

On thy rock rooted virtue firmly seated sublime,

Below thee break harmlefs the billows of time :

The ftrip'd flag fhall wave ftill and glory enfue,

And freedom find ev - er a guardian in you.

CHORO GRANDO.

Huz - - za ! Huz - - za ! Huz - - za ! for

brave A-mer-i - - ca,   where freedom fecures,

For a high. car of creft, blazon'd glory are yours.

Let Spain boaſt the treaſures that grow in her mines,
Let Gallia rejoice in her olives and wines;
In bright ſparkling jewels let India prevail,
With her odours, Arabia, perfuming ev'ry gale:
'Tis America alone that can boaſt of the ſoil,
Where the fair fruits of virtue and liberty ſmile.
 Huzza for brave America, where freedom ſecures,
 For the bleſſings of virtue and plenty are yours.

Our boſoms in raptures beat high at thy name,
Thy health is our tranſport—our triumph, thy fame:
Like our ſires, with our ſwords, we'll ſupport thy re-
 nown;
What they bought with their blood we'll defend
 with our own.
Smile ye Guardians of Freedom your brave ſons im-
 plore,
That America may flouriſh till time be no more.
 Huzza, &c.
For the bleſſings of peace and large commerce are yours.

The muſes to thee a glad tribute ſhall pay,
We flouriſh with freedom, with freedom decay,
Our hearts faintly murmur, or ſilently ſtand,
Should the ſword of oppreſſion 'gain wave o'er our
 land.
Can the Eagle ſoar high, Can ſhe dart like the wind,
When her files are oppreſt, and her pinions confin'd?
  Huzza, &c.
For a Bowdoin, a Lincoln and Adams are yours.

With fweetnefs and beauty thy daughters arife,
With rofe blooming che ks and love languifhing eyes
Hafte ye Graces, cries Venus, to America repair,
Fit conforts for heroes, the firft of the fair :
For to whom fhould the bleffings of freedom defcend,
But to fons of thofe fires who dar'd freedom defend.

Huzza for brave America, where freedom fecures,
For a HANCOCK, FRANKLIN and WASHINGTON
    are yours.

SONG XLVIII.

FRESH AND STRONG.

Frefh and ftrong the breeze is   blowing,

While yon fhip at   an - chor rides ; Sullen

K 2

waves in - cef - fant flowing, Rudely dafh

a - gainft her fides ; Thus my heart its

courfe im - ped - ed, Beats in my per-

turbed breaft ; Doubts like waves by

waves fuc - ceed-ed, Rife, and ftill de-

ny me reft.

Cruel phantoms rife nocturnal,
    Paint a dreadful fcene to come ;
Haunt my foul each hour diurnal—
    Chide AMANDA's wifh to roam :
Yet a ray of hope beams on me,
    Still AMANDA may be kind ;
Why fhould fancy's vifions vex me—
    Mere delufions of the mind.

By her anchor ftill fupported,
    Idly round the tempeft roar :
See the broken cable parted,
    And, alas; the fhip's off fhore.
Thus defpair my foul annoying,
    Like an overwhelming wave ;
Hope and fear alike deftroying,
    Speed me to the filent grave.

SONG XLIX.

THE COTTAGER.

As on a lonely hill I ſtray'd, A cottage

in a vale I ſpy'd, Whereat I ne'er had been;

I being loſt from town to town, It being

late and the ſun was down, I call'd to

be let in.

A young and pretty cottager
Came tripping fingly to the door,
  Who did my foul delight ;
I urg'd my cafe, and my diftrefs,
She would not grant me my requeft :
  I turn'd, bid her good night.

The gloomy clouds o'erfpread the fky,
And all the whiftling winds blew high,
  As I to wander went :
So foft compaffion feiz'd her foul,
She could not bear to fee me ftroll,
  She call'd and gave confent.

Ye Gods of every charming grace,
Her lordly form and pretty face,
  I to the world prefer ;
And if fhe learns to love like me,
My glory e'er after fhall be
  My charming cottager.

SONG L.

AN ODE FOR THE FOURTH OF JULY.

Come all ye sons of song, Pour the full sound along

In joyful strains;   Beneath these western skies,

See a new empire rife, Burfting with glad furprife

Ty - ran-nic chains.

Liberty with keen eye,
Pierc'd the blue vaulted fky,
Refolv'd us free;

From her Imperial feat,
Beheld the bleeding ftate,
Approv'd this day's debate
    And firm decree.

Sublime in awful form,
Above the whirling ftorm,
    The Goddefs ftood ;
She faw with pitying eye,
War's tempeft raging high,
Our hero's bravely die,
    In fields of blood.

High on his fhining car,
Mars, the ftern God of war,
    Our ftruggles bleft :
Soon victory wave her hand,
Fair Freedom cheer'd the land,
Led on Columbia's band
    To glorious reft.

Now all ye fons of fong,
Pour the full found along,
    Who fhall control ;
For in this weftern clime,
Freedom fhall rife fublime,
Till ever changing time,
    Shall ceafe to roll.

SONG LI.

WRITTEN BY THOMAS DAWES, JUN. ESQUIRE, AND SUNG AT THE ENTERTAINMENT GIVEN, ON BUNKER's HILL, BY THE PROPRIETORS OF CHARLES RIVER BRIDGE, AT THE OPENING OF THE SAME.

To the foregoing Tune.

NOW let rich mufie found,
And all the region round,
 With rapture fill ;
Let the fhrill trumpet's fame,
To heaven itfelf proclaim,
The everlafting name,
 Of Bunker's hill ;

Beneath his fky rapt brow,
What heroes fleep below,
 How dear to Jove :
Not more belov'd were thofe,
Who foil'd celeftial foes,
When the old giants rofe
 To arms above.

Now fcarce eleven fhort years,
Have roll'd their rapid fpheres,
 Thro' heav'n's high road,
Since o'er yon fwelling tide,
Pafs'd all the Britifh pride,
And water'd Bunker's fide
 With foreign blood.
L

Then Charleſtown's gilded ſpires,
Met unrelenting fires,
   And ſunk in night :
But Phenix like they'll rife,
In columns to the ſkies,
And ſtrike the aſtoniſh'd eyes
   With glories bright.

Meand'ring to the deep,
Majeſtic Charles ſhall weep,
   Of war no more ;
Fam'd as the Appian way,
The world's firſt BRIDGE today,
All nation's ſhall convey,
   From ſhore to ſhore.

On this bleſt mountain's head,
The feſtive board we'll ſpiead,
   With viands high ;
Let joy's broad bowl go round,
With public ſpirit crown'd,
And conſecrate the ground
   To liberty.

SONG LII.

THE SAILOR BOY CAPERING ASHORE.

Poll, dang' it, how d'ye do ? Nan won't you g'us

a buſs ? Why, what's to do wi' you, Why here's a

pretty fuſs, Why, what's to do wi' you, Why

here's a pretty fuſs, Say, ſhall we kiſs and toy ?

I goes to ſea no more—Oh! I'm the sailor

boy, For capering a - ſhore, Oh! I'm the

ſailor boy, For capering a-ſhore.

Father he apprentic'd me,
All to a coafting fhip,
I b'ing refolv'd, d'ye fee,
To give 'em all the flip;
I got to Yarmouth Fair,
Where I had been before,
So father found me there,
A capering afhore.

Next out to India,
I went a Guinea pig,
We got to Table Bay,
But mind a pretty rig,
The fhip driv'n out to fea,
Left me and many more,
Among the Hottentots
A capering afhore.

I love's a bit of hop,
Life's ne'er the worfer for't,
If in my wake fhould drop,
A fiddle, "That's your fort,"
Thrice tumble up ahoy,
Once get the labour o'er,
Then fee the failor boy,
A capering afhore.

SONG LIII.

THE SAILOR's CONSOLATION.

Spanking Jack was so comely, so pleasant, so

jolly, Though wind blew great guns still he'd

whistle and sing. Jack lov'd his friend and

was true to his Molly, And if honour

gives greatness was great as a king. One night

as we drove with two reefs in the mainsail, And

L 2

the ſcud came on lowring up - on a lee-ſhore,

Jack went up aloft   for   to hand

the top ga'nt-ſail,   A   ſpray waſh'd him off

and we ne'er ſaw   him more ! we ne'er ſaw

him more ! But   grieving's   a   fol - ly,

Come let us be   Jolly, If we've troubles at

ſea, boys, We've pleaſures aſhore.

Whiffling Tom ftill of mifchief or fun in the middle
Through life in all weathers at random would jog,
He'd dance and he'd fing, and he'd play on the fiddle,
And fwig with an air his allowance of grog :
Long fide of a don in the Terrible Frigate
As yard arm and yard arm we lay off the fhore,
In and out whiffling Tom did fo caper and jig it,
That his head was fhot off, and we ne'er faw him more !
    But grieving's a folly, &c.

Bonny Ben was to each jolly meffmate a brother,
He was manly and honeft, good natured, and free,
If ever one tar was more true than another
To his friend and his duty, that failor was he ;
One day with the David to heave the kedge anchor,
Ben went in the boat on a bold craggy fhore,
He overboard tipt, when a fhark, and a fpanker,
Soon nipt him in two, and we ne'er faw him more !
    But grieving's a folly, &c.

But what of it all, lads, fhall we be down hearted
Becaufe that mayhap we now take our laft fup :
Life's cable muft one day or other be parted,
And death in faft mooring will bring us all up :
But 'tis always the way on't, one fcarce finds a brother
Fond as pitch, honeft, hearty and true to the core,
But by battle or ftorm or fome bad thing or other,
He's popp'd off the hooks, and we ne'er fee him more !
    But grieving's a folly, &c.

SONG LIV.

THE HEAVING OF THE LEAD.

For England when with fav'ring gale,

Our gallant ship up chan-nel fteer'd ; And

fcud-ding un-der   ea - fy fail, The high

blue weftern   land appear'd : To heave the

Lead the   feaman fprung, And to the   pi-

lot cheer - ly fung, BY THE DEEP NINE !

BY THE DEEP NINE ! To heave the lead the

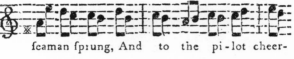

seaman sprung, And   to   the   pi-lot cheer-

ly fung, BY THE DEEP NINE!

And bearing up, to gain the port,
    Some well known object kept in view,
An abbey tow'r, an harbour fort:
    Or beacon, to the veffel true,
While oft the Lead the feaman flung,
    And to the pilot cheerly fung;
" BY THE MARK SEVEN."

And as the much lov'd fhore we near,
    With tranfport we beheld the roof
Where dwelt a friend or partner dear,
    Of faith and love a matchlefs proof.
The Lead once more the feaman flung,
    And to the watchful pilot fung,

" QUARTER LESS FIVE."

SONG LV.

AN ODE FOR THE FOURTH OF JULY.

By Daniel George.——Set to music by Horatio Garnet.

'Tis done! the edict paft, by Heav'n de-

creed, And *Han - - - - - cock's* name confirms

the glor'ous deed. On this aufpicious morn

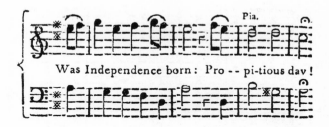

Was Independence born: Pro -- pi-tious day!

Hail the U-nit-ed States of bleft

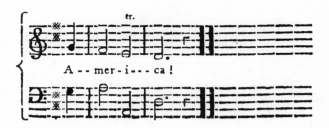

A -- mer - i --- ca!

THE AMERICAN

CHORUS.

Fortiſſimo.

Fly ! Fly ! Fly, ſwift wing'd Fame, The

ne - - - - - - - - ws, the news proclaim : From

ſhore to ſhore Let can-nons roar ; And

joy - - - ful   vo·c - - - es   fhout Co - lum-

bia's name,   fhout,   fhout   Columbia's name,

Co-lum-bia's name.

M

See haughty Britain, fending hofts of foes,
With vengeance arm'd, our freedom to oppofe ;
    But WASHINGTON, the Great,
    Difpell'd impending fate,
        And fpurn'd each plan :
Americans, combine to hail the godlike man.
        Fly, fwift-wing'd Fame, &c.

Let Saratoga's crimfon plains declare
The deeds of Gates, that " thunderbolt of war :"
    His trophies grac'd the field ;
    He made whole armies yield—
        A vet'ran band :
In vain did Burgoyne ftrive his valor to withftand.
        Fly, fwift-wing'd Fame, &c.

Now Yorktown's heights attract our wond'ring eyes,
Where loud artill'ry rends the lofty fkies :
    There WASHINGTON commands,
    With Gallia's chofen bands,
        A warlike train ;   (plain.
Like Homer's conq'ring gods, they thunder o'er the
        Fly, fwift-wing'd Fame, &c.

Pale terror marches on, with folemn ftride ;
Cornwallis trembles, Britain's boafted pride,
    He, and his armed hofts,
    Surrender all their pofts,
        To WASHINGTON,
The friend of Liberty, Columbia's fav'rite fon.
        Fly, fwift-wing'd Fame, &c.

Now from Mount Vernon's peaceful ſhades again,
The Hero comes, with thouſands in his train :
    'Tis WASHINGTON, the Great
    Muſt fill the chair of ſtate,
        Columbia cries :
Each tongue the glorious name re-echoes to the ſkies.
        Fly, ſwift-wing'd Fame, &c.

Now ſhall the uſeful arts of peace prevail,
And commerce flouriſh, favor'd by each gale ;
    Diſcord, forever ceaſe,
    Let Liberty and Peace,
        And Juſtice reign ;
For WASHINGTON protects the ſcientific train.
        Fly, ſwift-wing'd Fame, &c.

SONG LVI.

HER ABSENCE WILL NOT ALTER ME.

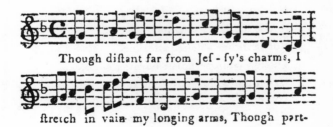

Though diſtant far from Jeſ - ſy's charms, I

ſtretch in vain my longing arms, Though part-

ed by the depths of fea, Her abfence fhall not

al - ter me. Tho' beaut'ous nymphs I fee a-

round, A Chloris, Flo - ra, might be found, Or

Phil - lis with her rov - ing eye : Her abfence

fhall not al - - ter me.

A fairer face, a fweeter fmile,
Inconftant lovers may beguile,
But to my lafs I'll conftant be,
Nor fhall her abfence alter me.
Though laid on India's burning coaft,
Or on the wide Atlantic toft,
My mind from love no pow'r could free,
Nor could her abfence alter me.

See how the flow'r that courts the fun
Purfues him till his race is run !
See how the needle feeks the Pole,
Nor diftance can its pow'r controul !
Shall lifelefs flow'rs the fun purfue,
The needle to the Pole prove true :
Like them fhall I not faithful be,
Or fhall her abfence alter me ?

Afk, who has been the turtle dove
Unfaithful to its marrow prove ?
Or who the bleating ewe has feen
Defert his lambkin on the green ?
Shall beaft and birds, inferior far
To us, difplay their love and care ?
Shall they in union fweet agree,
And fhall her abfence alter me ?

For conqu'ring love is ftrong as death,
Like vehement flames his pow'rful breath,
Thro' floods unmov'd his courfe he keeps,
Ev'n thro' the fea's devouring deeps :
His vehement flames my bofom burn,
Unchang'd they blaze till thy return :
My faithful Jeffy then fhall fee,
Her abfence has not alter'd me.

M 2

SONG LVII.

COME ROUSE BROTHER SPORTSMAN.

Come roufe, brother fportfman, The hunters

all cry, We've got a ftrong fcent, and a fa-vor-

ing fky, We've got a ftrong fcent, we've got

a ftrong fcent, we've got a ftrong fcent and

a favoring fky. The horn's fprightly notes,

And the lark's early fong, Will chide the dull

fportfman for fleeping fo long, Will chi - - - -

de, Will chide the dull

sportsman for sleeping so long, Will chide the

dull sportsman for sleeping so long.

Bright Phœbus has shewn us the glimpse of his face,
Peep'd in at our windows and call'd to the chace,
He soon will be up, for his dawn wears away,
And makes the fields blush with the beams of his ray,
Sweet Molly may teaze you perhaps to lie down,
And if you refuse her, perhaps she may frown;
But tell her sweet love must to hunting give place,
For as well as her charms, there are charms in the
    chace.

Look yonder, look yonder, old Reynard I spy,
And his brush nimbly follows brisk Chanter and Fly:

They feize on their prey, fee his eye balls they roll,
We're in at the death, now go home to the bowl.
There we'll fill up our glaffes and toaft to the king,
From a bumper frefh loyalty ever will fpring,
To George, peace and glory may heavens difpenfe,
And fox-hunters flourifh a thoufand years hence.

SONG LVIII.

THE RACE HORSE.

Allegretto.

See the courfe throng'd with gazers, the
fports are be - gun, The con - fu - fion but
hear, I bet you fir, done, done, Ten
thoufand ftrange murmurs re - found far
and near, Lords, hawk-ers and jockies af-

fail the tir'd   car, Lords, hawkers and

jockies af - fail the tir'd car, While with

neck like a   rain-bow e - rect - ing his

creft, Pamper'd, prancing and pleas'd, his head

touching his breaft, Scarcely   fnuffing

the air he's fo proud and e - late,

The high mettled   rac - er firft ftarts for

the plate, The   high   mettled   racer, The

high   mettled   racer firft ftarts for the plate.

Now Reynard's turn'd out, and o'er hedge and ditch
   rufh,
Dogs, horfes and huntfman all hard at his brufh ;
Thro' marfh, fen and briar led by their fly prey.
They by fcent and by view cheat a long tedious way :
While alike born for fports of the field and the courfe,
Always fure to come through—a ftaunch and fleet horfe.
When fairly run down, the fox yields up his breath,
The high mettled racer is in at the death.

Grown aged, us'd up and turn'd out of the ftud,
Lame, fpavin'd and wind gall'd—but yet with fome
   blood :
While knowing poftillions his pedigree trace,
Tell his dam won this fweepftakes, his fire that race,
And what matches he won, to the hoftlers count o'er,
As they loiter their time at fome hedge alehoufe door.
While the harnefs fore galls, and the fpurs his fides
   goad,
The high mettled racer's a hack on the road.

Till at laft having labour'd, drudg'd early and late,
Bow'd down by degrees, he bends on to his fate ;

Blind, old, lean and feeble, he tugs round a mill,
Or draws fand till the fand of his hour glafs ftands ftill.
And now cold and lifelefs, expofed to the view,
In the very fame cart which he yefterday drew ;
While a pitying croud his fad relics furrounds,
The high mettled racer is fold for the hounds.

SONG LIX.
ROMPING ROSY NELL.

Let ev'ry Pagan mufe be gone ; I feek no aid from Hel-i-con ;

Her locks auburne—her azure eyes,
Are fofter than the ethereal fkies :
But oh ! what daring pen can tell
The charms of romping rofy Nell ?

Aurora hides her blufhing face
When Nell appears, with heavenly grace !
And every nymph, of hill and dell,
Envies the romping rofy Nell.

Not all Arabia's fpicy coaft
Affords fuch fweets as Nell can boaft—
Why pants my heart—I dare not tell—
I figh for romping rofy Nell !

N

SONG LX.

THE GRACEFUL MOVE.

Air. Largo.

When first I saw thee, Graceful Move,

Ah me! what meant my throbbing breast?

Say, soft con - fu-fion, Art thou love?

If love thou art, then farewell reft.

With gentle fmiles affuage the pain
Thofe gentle fmiles did firft create,
And tho' you cannot love again,
In pity, ah! forbear to hate.

SONG LXI.

I SIGH FOR THE GIRL I ADORE.

ANDANTINO.

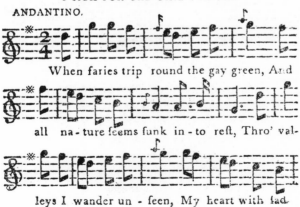

When faries trip round the gay green, And
all na-ture feems funk in-to reft, Thro' val-
leys I wander un-feen, My heart with fad-

sorrow op-prest : Then oft by the

murmuring, murmuring streams, Fair Elean-

or's loss I deplore, As a-lone by the

moon's, the moon's silver beams, I sigh, I

sigh, I sigh for the girl I adore.

When my flocks wander o'er the wide plain,
  To some thicket of woodbine I rove ;
There I pensively tune some soft strain,
  Or sing forth the praise of my love :
Where does my fair Eleanor stray,
  Must I ne'er see the nymph any more :
Thus distracted, I mourn the long day,
  And sigh for the girl I adore.

When firſt I beheld the ſweet maid,
  By moonlight, alone in the vale;
Far, far from the village we ſtray'd,
  Where I tenderly told the ſoft tale :
How long muſt I wander forlorn,
  Ah! when will my ſorrows be o'er;
Such grief it can never be borne ;
  I ſigh for the girl I adore.

SONG LXII.

HOW BLEST HAS MY TIME BEEN.

How bleſt has my time been, what joys
have I known, Since wedlock's ſoft bondage
made Jeſ - - - ſy my own: So joyful my
heart is, ſo ea - ſy my chain, That freedom

N 2

is taftelefs, and rov - - ing a pain.

Thro' walks grown with woodbines as often we ftray,
Around us our boys and girls frolic and play :
How pleafing their fport is ! the wanton ones fee,
And borrow their looks from my Jeffy and me.

To try her fweet temper, oft times am I feen,
In revels all day with the nymphs on the green :
Tho' painful my abfence, my doubts fhe beguiles,
And meets me at night with complaifance and fmiles.

What tho' on her cheeks the rofe lofes its hue,
Her wit and good humour blooms all the year-thro' :
Time ftill, as he flies, adds increafe to her truth,
And gives to her mind what he fteals from her youth.

Ye fhepherds fo gay, who make love to enfnare,
And cheat with falfe vows the too credulous fair,
In fearch of true pleafure how vainly you roam,
To hold it for life you muft find it at home.

SONG LXIII.

THE JOLLY SAILOR.

When my fortune does frown, I'll not be caſt

down, Repining wont al - ter my ſtore : But a

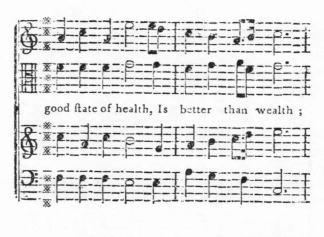

good ſtate of health, Is better   than wealth ;

I'll be merry although I am   poor.

I'll be merry although I am poor.

The foldier delights,
In blood, wars and fights,
    The failor to fail the feas o'er :
While this mind I'm in,
I'll keep a full fkin :
    I'll be merry, &c.

When the failors drink wine,
Their lovers repine :
    The mifer is fond of his ftore,
Give me but one quart,
Juft to comfort my heart,
    I'll be merry, &c.

Ye benevolent fouls,
With full flowing bowls,
    Who cheerfully add to the ftore :

Give the glutton his diſh,
And me what I wiſh,
    I'll be merry, &c.

And ye drunken ſots,
Who call for your pots,
    And ever are calling for more :
Only juſt let me drink,
And I'll make you all think,
    I'll be merry, &c.

SONG LXIV.

THE DESPONDING NEGRO.

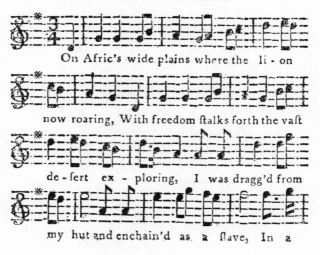

On Afric's wide plains where the li - on

now roaring, With freedom ſtalks forth the vaſt

de - ſert ex - ploring, I was dragg'd from

my hut and enchain'd as a ſlave, In a

dark floating dungeon up--on the salt

wave, Spare a halfpenny, Spare a halfpenny,

Spare a halfpenny to a poor Negro.

Tofs'd on the wild main, I all wildly defpairing,
Burft my chains rufh'd on deck with my eyeballs
    glaring,   (day,
When the lightnings dread blaft ftruck the inlets of
And its glorious bright beams fhut forever away.
    Spare a halfpenny, &c.

The defpoiler of man then his profpect thus lofing,
Of gain by my fale, not a blind bargain choofing,
As my value compar'd with my keeping was light,
Had me dafh'd overboard in the dead of night.
    Spare a halfpenny, &c.

And but for a bark to Britannia's coaft bound then,
All my cares by that plunge in the deep had been
    drown'd then,   (wave,
But by moonlight defcry'd, I was fnatch'd from the
And reluctantly robb'd of a watery grave.
    Spare a halfpenny, &c.

How difaftrous my fate, freedom's ground tho' I tread
   now,   (bread now,
Torn from home, wife and children, and wand'ring for
While feas roll between us which ne'er can be crofs'd,
And hope's diftant glimm'rings in darknefs are loft.

   Spare a halfpenny, &c.

But of minds foul and fair when the judge and the
   ponderer,   (derer,
Shall reftore light and reft to the blind and the wan-
'The European's deep dye may outrival the floe,
And the foul of an Erhiop prove white as the fnow.

   Spare a halfpenny, &c.

SONG LXV.

SWEET LILIES OF THE VALLEY.

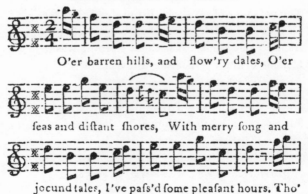

O'er barren hills, and   flow'ry dales, O'er

feas and diftant fhores, With merry fong and

jocund tales, I've pafs'd fome pleafant hours. Tho'

wand'ring thus, I ne'er could find, A girl like

blithfome Sally—Who picks, and culls, and cries

aloud, Who picks, and culls, and cries aloud,

Sweet Lilies of the Valley, Sweet Lilies

of the Valley, Who picks, and culls, and cries

aloud, Sweet Lilies of the Valley.

From whiftling o'er the harrow'd turf,
  From nefting of each tree,
I chofe a foldier's life to wed,
  So focial, gay, and free :
O

Yet, tho' the laſſes love as well,
    And often try to rally,
None pleaſes me like her who cries—
    Sweet Lilies of the Valley.

I'm now return'd, of late diſcharg'd,
    To uſe my native toil—
From fighting in my country's cauſe,
    To plough my country's ſoil :
I care not which, with either pleas'd,
    So I poſſeſs my Sally,
That little merry nymph, who cries
    Sweet Lilies of the Valley.

SONG LXVI.

DEAR LITTLE COTTAGE MAIDEN.

From place to place I travers'd long, Devoid of care or ſorrow, With lightſome heart and merry ſong, I thought not of tomorrow.

But when Priſcilla caught my eye, With ev'ry

charm array'd in, I ſigh'd and ſung, I know

not why, Dear   little   Cottage Maiden, Dear

little   Cottage   Maiden, Dear little   Cottage

Maiden,   I ſigh'd and ſung, I know not why,

Dear   little   Cottage Maiden, Dear   little

Cottage   Maiden.

And would the charmer be but mine,
  Sweet nymph, I'd fo revere thee ;
I'd gladly fhare my fate with thine,
  And evermore be near thee.
Tho' gold may pleafe the proud and great,
  My heart with love is laden,
Then let us join in wedlock's ftate,
  Dear little Cottage Maiden.

O'er me and mine, come miftrefs prove,
  And then, what ill can harm us,
Kind hymen will each fear remove,
  And fpread each fweet to charm us :
Together we will live content,
  And nought but love will trade in,
So fweetly fhall our lives be fpent,
  Dear little Cottage Maiden.

SONG LXVII.

SOMEBODY.

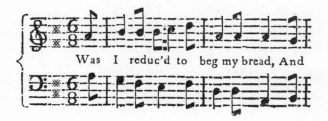

Was I reduc'd to beg my bread, And

had not where to lay my head, I'd creep

where yonder herds are fed, And steal a l ok

at some-bo-dy, My own dear some-bo-

dy, My conſtant some-bo-dy, I'd creep

where yon-der herds are fed, And steal a look

at some-bo-dy.

When I'm laid low, and am at reſt,
And maybe number'd with the bleſt,
Say will thy artleſs feeling breaſt
Throb with regard for—ſomebody :
  Thy own dear ſomebody—
  Thy conſtant ſomebody.
Ah ! will you drop the pitying tear,
And ſigh for the loſt—ſomebody ?

But ſhould I ever live to ſee
That form ſo much ador'd by me,
Then thou'lt reward my conſtancy,
And I'll be bleſt with—ſomebody :
  My own dear ſomebody—
  My conſtant ſomebody.
Then ſhall my tears be dri'd by thee,
And I'll be bleſt with—ſomebody.

SONG LXVIII.

FOREVER FORTUNE.

Forever, Fortune wilt thou prove An un-

relenting foe to love? And when we meet a

mutual heart, Come in between and bid us part?

Bid us figh on, from day to day, And wifh and

wifh our fouls away, Till youth and genial years

are flown, And all the life of life is gone.

But bufy, bufy ftill art thou
    To bind the lovelefs, joylefs vow ;
The heart from pleafure to delude,
    To bind the gentle with the rude.

For once, O Fortune, hear my pray'r,
    And I abfolve thy future care ;
All other bleffings I refign,
    Make but the dear Amanda mine.

SONG LXIX.

THE CHARMING CREATURE.

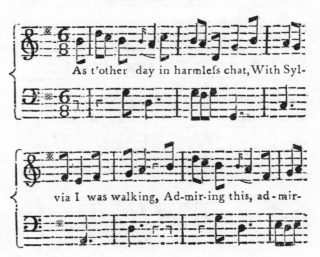

As t'other day in harmlefs chat, With Syl-

via I was walking, Ad-mir-ing this, ad-mir-

ing that, To-gether fweetly talking ; Young

Damon met us   in the grove, With joy in

ev'ry feature ; He prefs'd my hand, then whif-

per'd love, O what a charming creature !

O what a charming creature!

His paſſion oft times he expreſs'd,
    In words ſo ſoft and kind,
I felt a ſomething in my breaſt,
    But doubts were in my mind.
I told him he with Doll was ſeen,
    And ſure he came to meet her ;
He vow'd I was his only queen,
    O what a charming creature !

To yonder church, then ſhall we go?
    He preſt me to comply ;
(How can the men thus teaze one ſo ?)
    I try'd from him to fly :
And will my Delia name the day ?
    Let Damon kindly greet her?
Thus cloſely preſt, what could I ſay
    To ſuch a charming creature !

SONG LXX.

THE UNHAPPY SWAIN.

Ceafe ye fountains, ceafe to murmur, Balmy

winds your breath forbear : Gent - ly flowing,

foft - ly blowing Zephyrs wake your

ten - der care.

Gentle nymph, affuage my anguifh,
    At your feet a humble fwain ;
Prays you would not fee him languifh,
    One kind look would foothe my pain.

Did you know the lad who courts you,
    He not long would fue in vain ;
Prince of fong, and dance, and fport, you
    Scarce can meet the like again.

By his fighs you may difcover,
    What fond wifhes touch his heart ;
Eyes can fpeak, and tell the lover,
    What the tongue cannot impart.

Ah ! my Delia, muft I leave thee,
    Can my foul fuch pains endure ;
Think, oh ! think how parting grieves me,
    Nought on earth affords a cure.

Muft thefe eyes no more behold thee,
    Drefs'd in ev'ry blooming grace ;
Muft thefe arms no more enfold thee ;
    Muft a phantom fill the place.

Blufhing fhame forbids revealing,
    What the heart muft difapprove ;
But 'tis hard, and paft concealing,
    When we truly, fondly, love.

If 'tis joy to wound a lover,
   How much more, to give him eafe ;
When his paffion you difcover,
   Oh ! how pleafing 'tis to pleafe.

SONG LXXI.

THE STREAMLET THAT FLOW'D ROUND HER COT.

AFFETTUOSO.

The ftreamlet that flow'd round her cot, All

the charms, All the charms of my Em-i-ly knew :

How oft has its courfe been forgot, While it

paus'd, While it paus'd her dear image to woo.

paus'd her dear image to woo.

P

Believe me, the fond filver tide,
    Knew from whence it deriv'd the fair prize,
For filently fwelling with pride,
    It reflected it back to the fkies.

SONG LXXII.
THE BEE.

As Cupid in a garden ftray'd

tranf-port-ed with the damafk fhade :

A lit - tle BEE, un - feen, a-

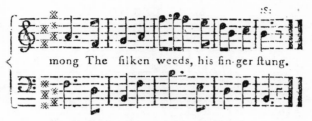

mong The filken weeds, his fin-ger ftung.

The tears his beauteous cheeks ran down,
He ftorm'd, he blow'd the burning wound ;
Then flying to a neighbouring grove,
Thus plantive told the Queen of Love,

Ah! ah, mama, ah me, I die,
A little infect, wing'd to fly ;
Its call'd a B E E, on yonder plain,
It ftung me, oh ! I die with pain !

Then V E N U S mildly thus rejoin'd,
If you, my dear, fuch anguifh find,
From the refentment of a B E E,
Think what thofe feel, who're ftung by thee.

SONG LXXIII.

SOPHRONIA.

Forbear my friends, forbear and afk no

more, Where all my cheerful airs are fled;

Why will ye make me talk my torments

o'er,   My life, my joy, my comfort's dead.

Deep from my foul, mark how the fobs arife,
   Hear the long groans that wafte my breath ;
And read the mighty forrows in my eyes,
   Lovely Sophronia fleeps in death.

Unkind difeafe, to veil that rofy face,
   With tumors of a mortal pale ;
While mortal purples. with their difmal grace,
   And double terrors fpot the veil.

Uncomely veil, and moft unkind difeafe,
   Is this Sophronia once fo fair ?
Are thefe the features that were born to pleafe,
   And beauty fpread her enfigns there ?

I was all love, and fhe was all delight,
   Let me run back to feafons paft ;
Ah ! flow'ry days, when firft fhe charm'd my fight,
   But rofes will not always laft.

But still SOPHRONIA pleas'd, not time nor care,
    Could take her youthful bloom away ;
Virtue has charms, which nothing can impair,
    Beauty like hers could ne'er decay.

Grace is a sacred plant, of heavenly birth,
    The feed descending from above,
Roots in a soil refin'd, grows high on earth,
    And blooms with life, and joy, and love.

Such was SOPHRONIA's soil, celestial dew
    And angels food, was her repast ;
Devotion was her work, and thence she drew
    Delight which strangers never taste.

Not the gay splendor of a flatt'ring court,
    Could tempt her to appear and shine ;
Her solemn airs forbid the world resort,
    But I was blest, for she was mine.

Safe on her welfare, all my pleasures hung,
    Her smiles could all my pains controul ;
Her soul was made of softness, and her tongue
    Was soft and gentle as her soul.

She was my guide, my friend, my earthly all,
    Love grew with every waning moon ;
Had heav'n, a length of years delay'd to call
    Still I had thought it call'd too soon.

But peace, my forrows, nor with murmuring voice,
  Dare to accufe heaven's high decree ;
She was firft ripe for everlafting joys,
  SOPHRON, fhe waits above for thee.

SONG LXXIV.

THE MUSICAL SOCIETY.

Well met my loving friends of art, Let

us in concert fing ; And let each bear his

vocal part, And tuneful voices ring : Each

join with me his well tun'd harp, In concert sweet

I   say ;   And let us key on either sharp,

And sing, sol, la, me   fa.

Let Will and John the Tenor sound,
    And sing melodiously ;
While Ben and Jo, the Bass do ground,
    To make sweet harmony :
Let George and James sing Counter sweet,
    In chords that sweetly play ;
To move all parts, soft and complete,
    We'll sing sol, la, mi, fa.

Within the temple Solomon,
  In muſic took delight ;
And voices had, to join as one,
  Two hundred eighty eight :
Then may we ever take delight,
  In muſic's art, alway ;
And we'll unite, both day and night,
  To ſing ſol, la, mi, fa.

Remember holy David well,
  In muſic's art was vers'd :
His voice and harp, could ſpirits quell,
  For Saul he diſpoſſeſs'd :
Each join with me his well tun'd harp,
  In concert ſweet I ſay ;
And ſet your key on either ſharp,
  And ſing ſol, la, mi, fa.

SONG LXXV.

ODE FOR THE NEW YEAR.

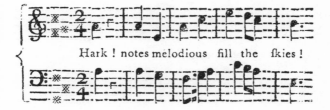

Hark ! notes melodious fill the ſkies !

'From Thetis' lap, Apollo rife ! 'Thy swift

wheel'd chariot speed, 'Thy swift wheel'd chariot

speed amain ! 'O'er   fleeting courfers,

fleeting courfers loofe the rein ! 'The blufh-

ing hours, 'The bluſhing hours im - - - pa-

tient ſtand! 'The vir-gin day waits thy

com-mand!

CHORUS.

'Awake, O Sol! And 'ead from ether's

" And as the golden car of light,
' Refulgent beams on mortal fight ;
' As fiery fteeds (which oft times lave
' Their winged feet in ocean's wave)
' Afcend above the mantling deep,
' And rapid gain th' empyrean fteep,
   " Let flumb'ring nations rife, and loud prolong,
   " To Day's celeftial Prince, the choral fong."

Columbia head the high beheft,
Her free born millions fmote the breaft !
And filent flept the heav'n ftrung lyre,
Till Freedom breath'd impaffion'd fire ;
Till Virtue form'd the hallow'd found,
And Fame enraptur'd roll'd it round.
   " All hail to Freedom's, Virtue's, Glory's Son !
   " Ye worlds repeat, repeat ! 'Tis WASHINGTON."

European kingdoms caught the ftrain,
From mount to vale—from hill to plain,
Triumphant fhouts with one acclaim,
Reechoing fwell'd the trump of Fame ;
All hail ! the Gallic peafant cries !
The cloifter'd monk, the nun replies !
   Illuftrious GEORGE ! Great Patriot Sage ! 'Twas thine !
   To pour on France, the flood of light divine !

Q

What notes are thefe ? How grand ! fublime ?
'Tis freedom's fong in *Afric's* clime !
The wretch, the flave whom fetters bound,
Exulting hears the joyful found ;
Ecftatick tranfports fire his foul,
And grateful pæans hourly roll ;
 For thee alone, he hails the rifing dawn ;
 The friend of man in WASHINGTON *was born.*

Lo, *Afia* joins the note of praife ;
Her myriads dream of halcyon days ;
When holy truth, with eagle ken,
Shall fcan the rights of fellow men ;
When impious Tyrants hurl'd from pow'r,
No more fhall fpoil induftry's flow'r ;
 But perfect Freedom gild her ev'ning Sun,
 And glow with cloudlefs beam---like WASHINGTON.

Hail favour'd land, the pride of earth !
All nations hail Columbia's birth ;
From Europe's realms, to Afia's fhore,
Or where the Niger's billows roar,
On Eagle plume thy deeds fhall fly ;
And long as Sol adorns the fky,
 Ten thoufand thoufand clarion tongues proclaim,
 The godlike WASHINGTON's *immortal name.*

Oh rapid poft ye rolling years !
Revolving fwift through circling fpheres,

And hafte along the promis'd time,
When liberty, from clime to clime,
With facred peace, and union join'd,
And virtue bleffing human kind,
   Shall equal blifs diffuse beneath the Sun,
   And ev'ry nation boaft a WASHINGTON.

SONG LXXVI.
MARY's DREAM.

The moon had clim'd the high - eft
hill, Which rif - es o'er the fource
of Dee, And from the eaftern

sum-mit shed Her sil-ver light on

tow'r and tree; When Mary laid her

down to sleep, Her thoughts on Sandy

far at sea, When soft and low a

voice was heard, Saying, Ma - ry weep

no   more   for   me.

She from her pillow gently rais'd
  Her head, to afk who there might be.
She faw young Sandy fhiv'ring ftand,
  With vifage pale and hollow eye ;
" O Mary dear, cold is my clay,
  " It lies beneath a ftormy fea,
" Far, far from thee, I fleep in death,
  " So Mary, weep no more for me.

" Three ftormy nights and ftormy days
  " We tofs'd upon the raging main :
" And long we ftrove our bark to fave,
  " But all our ftriving was in vain :

Q 2

" Ev'n then, when horror chill'd my blood,
  " My heart was fill'd with love for thee ;
" The storm is past, and I at rest,
  " So Mary, weep no more for me.

" O maiden dear, thyself prepare,
  " We soon shall meet upon that shore,
" Where love is free from doubt and care,
  " And thou and I shall part no more."
Loud crow'd the cock, the shadow fled,
  No more of Sandy could she see ;
But soft the passing spirit said,
  " Sweet Mary, weep no more for me."

SONG LXXVII.

MAJOR ANDRE.

Return en - rap - tur'd hours, When Delia's

heart was mine ; When she with wreaths of

flow'rs, My tem-ples did entwine, Not

jeal - ouf - y nor care, Cor - rod - ed

in my breaft ; But vifions light as

air, Pre-fid-ed o——'er my reft,.

Since I'm remov'd from ftate,
  And bid adieu to time,
At my unhappy fate
  Let DELIA not repine ;
But may the mighty JOVE,
  Her crown with happinefs !
This grant, ye powr's above !
  And take my foul to blifs !

Now nightly o'er my bed,
  No airy phantoms play ;
No flowrets deck my head,
  Each vernal holiday.
Far, far from the fad plain,
  The cruel DELIA flies,
While rack'd with jealous pain,
  Her wretched ANDRE dies,

SONG LXXVIII.

THEN SAY MY SWEET GIRL, CAN YOU LOVE ME?

Dear Nancy I've fail'd the world all

around, And seven long years been a

rover, To make for my charmer each

shilling a pound, But now my hard per-

ils are o-ver. I've fav'd from my toils ma-

ny hundreds of gold, The comforts of life

to beget ; Have borne in each climate, the heat and the cold, Have borne in each climate the heat and the cold, And all for my pretty bru- nette. Then fay my fweet girl, Can you love me ? Then fay my fweet girl, Can you love me ? Then fay my fweet girl, Can you love me ?

Tho' others may boaſt of more riches than mine,
  And rate my attractions e'en fewer,
At their jeers and ill nature I'll ſcorn to repine :
  Can they boaſt of a heart that is truer ?

Or will they for thee, plough the hazardous main—
    Brave the feafons both ftormy and wet ?
If not ; why, I'll do it again and again,
    And all for my pretty brunette.
        Then fay, &c.

When order'd afar, in purfuit of the foe,
    I figh'd at the bodings of fancy,
Which fain would perfuade me I might be laid low :
    And ah ! never more fee my Nancy.
But hope like an angel, foon banifh'd the thought,
    And bade me fuch nonfence forget ;
I took the advice, and undauntedly fought,
    And all for my pretty brunette.
        Then fay, &c.

SONG LXXIX.

HOMEWARD BOUND.

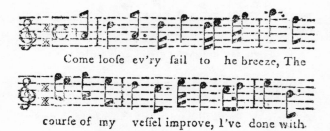

Come loofe ev'ry fail to he breeze, The

courfe of my   veffel improve, I've done with

the toils of the feas, Ye failors I'm bound

to my love, Ye failors I'm bound to my

love. Ye failors I'm bound to my love,

I've done with the toils of the feas,

Ye fail - ors I'm bound to my love.

Since EMMA is true as fhe's fair,
　My griefs I fling all to the wind;
'Tis a pleafing return for my care,
　My miftrefs is conftant and kind.

My fails are all fill'd to my dear,
　What tropic bird fwifter can move,
Who, cruel, fhall hold his career,
　When he's bound to the arms of his love.

Come, hoiſt ev'ry ſail to the breeze,
Come, ſhipmates, and join in the ſong,
Let's drink, while the ſhip cuts the ſeas,
To the gale that now wafts us along.

SONG LXXX.

THE HERMIT.

At the cloſe of the day, when the ham-

let was ſtill, And mortals the ſweets of for-

get-ful-neſs prove ; When nought but the

torrent was heard on the hill, And nought but

the nightingal's song in the grove. 'Twas then

by the cave of a mountain re - clin'd, The

Hermit, his nightly complaint juſt be-gan ;

R

Though mournful his voice, yet his heart

was refign'd, He thought as   a   fage, though

he felt like   a   man.

Ah why thus abandon'd to forrow and woe,
　Why thus lonely, Philomel flows thy fad ftrains ;
For furing fhall return, and a lover beftow,
　And thy bofom no trace of misfortune retain.
Yet if pity infpire thee, ah ! ceafe not thy lay,
　Mourn fweeteft complainer, man calls thee to mourn ;
O foothe him whofe pleafures like thine fade away,
　Full quickly they pafs, but they never return.

Now gliding remote on the verge of the sky,
   The moon half extingnish'd, her crefent difplays ;
But lately I mark'd when majeftic on high,
   She fhone, and the planets were loft in her blaze.
Roll on, thou fair orb, and with gladnefs purfue
   The path that conducts thee to glory again ;
But man's faded glory, no change fhall renew,
   Ah ! fools to exult in a glory fo vain.

Tis night, and the landfcape is lovely no more,
   I mourn not, ye woodlands, I mourn not for you ;
For morn is approaching, your charms to reftore,
   Perfum'd with frefh fragrance, and glitt'ring with
      dew.
Nor yet for the ravage of winter I mourn,
   Kind nature the embryo's bloffom fhall fave ;
But when fhall fpring vifit the mouldering urn,
   Oh ! when fhall it dawn on the night of the grave.

SONG LXXXI.

COLUMBIA—By Dr. DWIGHT.

Co-lum-bia, Columbia to   glory

a-rife, The queen of the earth, and the
child of the fkies; Thy genius commands thee'
with rapture behold, While a-ges on a-ges
thy fplendor unfold. Thy reign is the laft, and

the noblest of time, Most fruitful thy soil,

most in - vit-ing thy clime: Let the crimes of

the east, ne'er en-crim-son thy name, Be freedom

and science, and virtue, thy fame.

R 2

To conqueſt and ſlaughter let Europe aſpire ;
Whelm nations in blood, and wrap cities on fire ;
Thy heroes the rights of mankind ſhall defend,
And triumph purſue them, and glory attend.
A world is thy realm : for a world be thy laws,
Enlarg'd as thine empire, and juſt as thy cauſe ;
On freedom's broad baſis thy empire ſhall riſe,
Extend with the main, and diſſolve with the ſkies.

Fair ſcience her gates to thy ſons ſhall unbar,
And the eaſt ſee thy morn hide the beams of thy ſtar ;
New bards, and new ſages, unrivall'd ſhall ſoar
To fame unextinguiſh'd, when time is no more ;
To thee, the laſt refuge of virtue deſign'd,
Shall fly from all nations the beſt of mankind :
Here, grateful to heaven, with tranſport ſhall bring
Their incenſe, more fragrant than odors of ſpring,

Nor leſs ſhall thy fair ones to glory aſcend,
And genius and beauty in harmony blend ;
The graces of form ſhall awake pure deſire,
And the charms of the ſoul ever cheriſh the fire :
Their ſweetneſs unmingled, their manners refin'd,
And virtues bright image, inſtamp'd on the mind,
With peace, and ſoft rapture ſhall teach life to glow,
And light up a ſmile in the aſpect of woe.

Thy fleets to all regions thy pow'r ſhall diſplay,
The nations admire, and the ocean obey ;

Each fhore to thy glory its tribute unfold,
And the eaft and the fouth yield their fpices and gold.
As the day-fpring unbounded, thy fplendor fhall flow,
And earth's little kingdoms before thee fhall bow,
While the enfigns of union, in triumph unfurl'd,
Hufh the tumult of war, and give peace to the world.

Thus, as down a lone valley, with cedars o'erfpread,
From war's dread confufion I penfively ftray'd ;
The gloom from the face of fair heaven retir'd ;
The winds ceas'd to murmur ; the thunders expir'd ;
Perfumes, as of Eden, flow'd fweetly along,
And a voice, as of angels, enchantingly fung,
" Columbia, Columbia, to glory arife,
The queen of the world, and the child of the fkies."

SONG LXXXII.

ADAMS and LIBERTY—By T. Paine.

ALLEGRETTO.

Ye   fons of Co - lum - bia, who bravely

have fought, For thofe rights, which unftain'd from

your   Sires had   de-scend-ed, May you

long taste the blessings your   valour has

bought, And your sons reap   the   soil, which you

fathers   defended,   Mid the reign of

mild   peace, May your   nation in-

creafe, With the   glory   of Rome, and the

wifdom of Greece ;   And   ne'er may   the

fons   of COLUMBIA be flaves, While the

earth bears a plant, or the sea rolls its waves.

In a clime, whose rich vales feed the marts of the
    world,
 Whose shores are unshaken by *Europe's* commotion,
The *Trident* of Commerce should never be hurl'd,
  To incense the *legitimate* powers of the ocean.
      But should *Pirates* invade,
      Though in thunder array'd,
    Let your *cannon* declare the *free charter* of TRADE.

For ne'er shall the sons of COLUMBIA *be slaves.*
While the earth bears a plant, or the sea rolls its waves.

The fame of our arms, of our laws the mild sway,
 Had justly ennobled our nation in story,
Till the dark clouds of *Faction* obscur'd our young day,
 And envelop'd the sun of American glory.
   But let TRAITORS be told,
   Who their *Country* have sold,
  And barter'd their *God*, for his image in *gold*—

That ne'er will the sons of COLUMBIA *be slaves,*
While the earth bears a plant, or the sea rolls its waves.

While FRANCE her huge limbs bathes recumbent in
  blood,
 And *society's base* threats with wide dissolution ;
May PEACE, like the *Dove*, who return'd from the flood,
 Find an *Ark* of abode in our mild CONSTITUTION !
   But though PEACE is our aim,
   Yet the boon we disclaim,
  If bought by our SOV'REIGNTY, JUSTICE, or FAME.

For ne'er shall the sons of COLUMBIA *be slaves,*
While the earth bears a plant, or the sea rolls its waves.

Tis the fire of the *flint*, each American warms ;
 Let *Rome's* haughty victors beware of *collision !*
Let them bring all the vassals of *Europe* in arms,
 WE'RE A WORLD BY OURSELVES, and disdain a
  division !

While, with patriot pride,
To our LAWS we're allied,
No foe can fubdue us—no faction divide.

For ne'er fhall the fons of COLUMBIA *be flaves,*
While the earth bears a plant, or the fea rolls its waves.

Our mountains are crown'd with imperial *Oak*,
Whofe *roots,* like our *Liberties,* ages have nourifh'd
But long ere our nation fubmits to the yoke,
Not a *tree* fhall be left on the field where it flourifh'd.
Should *invafion* impend,
Every *grove* would defcend
From the *hill tops* they fhaded, our *fhores* to defend.

For ne'er fhall the fons of COLUMBIA *be flaves,*
While the earth bears a plant, or the fea rolls its waves.

Let our Patriots deftroy *Anarch's* peftilent *worm,*
Left our Liberty's *growth* fhould be check'd by *corro-*
fion ;
Then let clouds thicken round us, we heed not the
ftorm ;
Our realm fears no *fhock,* but the earth's own explo-
fion.
Foes affail us in vain,
Though their FLEETS *bridge* the main,
For our *altars* and *laws* with our lives we'll main-
tain !

And ne'er fhall the fons of COLUMBIA *be flaves,*
While the earth bears a plant, or the fea rolls its waves.

S

Should the TEMPEST of WAR overſhadow our land,
  Its bolts could ne'er rend FREEDOM's temple aſunder;
For, unmov'd, at its *portal*, would WASHINGTON ſtand,
    And repulſe, with his BREAST, *the aſſaults of his* THUN-
      DER !
        His *ſword*, from the ſleep
        Of its *ſcabbard*, would leap,
      And conduct, with its *point*, every *flaſh* to the deep.

For ne'er ſhall the ſons of COLUMBIA *be ſlaves,*
While the earth bears a plant, or the ſea rolls its waves.

Let FAME to the world ſound AMERICA's voice ;
  No INTRIGUE *can her ſons from their* GOVERNMENT
    ſever :
Her PRIDE *is her* ADAMS---*his* LAWS *are her* CHOICE,
  And ſhall flouriſh till LIBERTY *ſlumber forever !*
      Then unite, heart and hand,
      Like *Leonidas'* band,
    And ſwear to the GOD of the ocean and land,

That ne'er ſhall the ſons of COLUMBIA *be ſlaves,*
While the earth bears a plant, or the ſea rolls its waves.

To heaven a-bove thy fervent orifons are flown ;

The tender pray'r thou put'ft up there, Shall call

a guardian angel down, Shall call a guardian

an - gel down, To watch me in the battle.

My fafety thy fair truth fhall be,
    As fword and buckler ferving,
My life fhall be more dear to me,
    Becaufe of thy preferving.
Let peril come, let horror threat,
    Let thundr'ring cannons rattle,
I fearlefs feek the conflict's hea',
    Affur'd when on the wings of love,
        To heaven above, &c.

Enough—with that benignant fmile
    Some kindred God infpir'd thee,
Who faw thy bofom void of guile,
    Who wonder'd and admir'd thee :

lower'd,   the   rain down pour'd,   And   loud

the winds did   blow.

Then cafting round his eyes,
   Thus of his fate he did complain ;
Ye cruel rocks and fkies,
   Ye ftormy feas, and angry main.:
What 'tis to mifs a lover's blifs,
   Alas, ye do not know ;
Make me your wreck, as I come back,
   But fpare me as I go.

Lo yonder ftands the tow'r,
   Where my beloved Hero lies ;
And the appointed hour
   Make hafte, fhe fits with longing eyes
To his fond fuit, the Gods were mute,
   The billows anfwer'd no ;

Up to the fkies, the furges rife,
  But funk the youth as low.

Meanwhile the waiting maid,
  Divided 'twixt her fear and love ;
Now does his ftay upbraid,
  Now dreads he fhould the paffage prove :
Oh ! faith, faid fhe, not heav'n nor thee,
  Our love fhall e'er divide ;
I'd leap this wall, could I but fall,
  By my Leander's fide.

Although the rifing fun,
  Did to his fight reveal, too late,
His Hero was undone ;
  Not by Leander's fuit, but fate :
Said fhe, I'll fhow, though we were two,
  Our vows were ever one ;
This proof I'll give, I will not live,
  Nor fhall he die alone.

Down from the wall fhe lept,
  Into the raging fea to him ;
Courting each wave fhe met,
  To teach her wearied arms to fwim :
The fea Gods wept, nor longer kept
  Her from her lover's fide ;
Then join'd at laft, fhe grafp'd him faft,
  They figh'd, embrac'd and dy'd.
          S 2

THE AMERICAN
SONG LXXXIV.

THE BEAUTIES OF FRIENDSHIP.

Young Myra is fair as fpring's

ear - ly flow - er, And Lau - ra

fings fweet as the bird in her bow'r;

Young My-ra is fair as fpring's early

flower, And Lau-ra sings sweet as the bird

in her bow'r; But friendship is fairer and

sweet - er than they, She looks like the

morning, and smiles like the day.

mild   peace, May your   nation   in-

creafe, With the   glory   of Rome, and the

wifdom of Greece ;   And   ne'er may   the

fons   of   COLUMBIA   be flaves, While the

an - gels vir-tues lay ; Too foon did heav'n af-

fert its claim, And call'd its own a-

way. And call'd its own a - way.

My An - na's worth, My An - na's charms Can

never more re-turn : Can never more re-

turn : What then can fill these widow'd arms ?

Ah,   me !   Ah, me !   Ah,

me ! my An-na's Urn.

Can I forget that blifs refin'd,
   Which bleft with her I knew ;
Our hearts in facred bonds entwin'd,
   Were bound by love too true :
That rural train which once was us'd,
   In feftive dance to turn ;
So pleas'd when Anna they amus'd,
   Now weeping deck her Urn.

The foul efcaping from its chain,
   She clafp'd me to her breaft ;
To part with thee is all my pain,
   She cried, then funk to reft :
While mem'ry fhall her feat retain,
   From beauteous Anna's Urn ;
My heart fhall breathe its ceafelefs ftrain,
   Of forrow o'er her Urn.

There with earlieft dawn, a dove,
   Laments her murder'd mate ;
There Philomela loft to love,
   Tells the pale moon her fate :
With yew and ivy round me fpread,
   My Anna there I'll mourn ;
For all my foul, now fhe is dead,
   Concenters in her Urn.

SONG LXXXVI.

CORYDON's GHOST—By Dr. N. DWIGHT.

What sorrowful sounds do I hear, Move

slowly along in the gale; How solemn they fall on

my ear, As softly they pass through the gale.

Sweet *Corydon's* notes are all o'er, Now lovely he

sleeps in the clay, His cheeks bloom with roſes no

more, Since death call'd his ſpirit a - way.

Sweet woodbines will riſe round his tomb,
    And willows there ſorrowing wave ;
Young hyacinths freſhen and bloom,
    While hauthons encircle his grave.
Each morn, when the ſun gilds the eaſt,
    The green graſs, beſpangled with dew,
Will caſt his bright beams to the weſt,
    To charm the ſad *Caroline*'s view.

O *Corydon*, hear the ſad cries,
    Of *Caroline*, plaintive and ſlow ;
O ſpirit, look down from the ſkies,
    And pity thy mourner below.

T

'Tis *Caroline*'s voice in the breeze,
  Which Philomel hears on the plain ;
Then ftriving the mourner to pleafe,
  In fympathy joins in her ftrain.

And when the ftill night has unfurl'd
  Her robe o'er the hamlets around,
Gray twilight retires from the world,
  And darknefs encumbers the ground ;
I'll leave my lone gloomy abode,
  To *Corydon's* urn will I fly ;
And kneeling will blefs the Juft God,
  Who dwells in bright manfion on high.

Ye fhepherds, fo blithefome and young,
  Retire from your fports on the green,
Since *Corydon's* deaf to my fong,
  The wolves tore his lambs on the plain.
Each fwain round the foreft will ftray,
  And forrowing hang down his head ;
His pipe then in fymphony play,
  Some dirge to young *Corydon's* fhade.

Since *Corydon* hears me no more,
  In gloom let the wood-lands appear ;
Ye oceans be ftill'd of your roar ;
  Let autumn extend round the year.
I'll hie me through meadow and lawn,
  There cull the bright flowrets of May ;
Then rife on the wings of the morn,
  And waft my young fpirit away.

SONG LXXXVII.

WITHIN A MILE OF EDINBURGH.

'Twas with-in a mile of Edinburgh town,

In the ro-fy time of the year, Sweet

flow-ers bloom'd, and the grafs was down,

And each fhepherd woed his dear : Bonny Joc-

key, blyth and gay, Kifs'd fweet Jenny making

hay : The laffie blufh'd, and frowning cry'd, No,

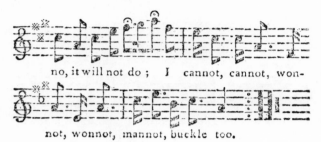

no, it will not do ;   I   cannot, cannot, won-

not, wonnot, mannot, buckle too.

Jockey was a wag that never would wed,
   Tho' long he had follow'd the lafs,
Contented fhe earn'd and eat her brown bread,
   And merrily turn'd up the grafs :
     Bonny Jockey, blyth and free,
     Won her heart right merrily,
Yet ftill fhe blufh'd, and frowning cry'd, no, no, it will
   not do,
I cannot cannot, wonnot wonnot, mannot buckle too.

  But when he vow'd he wou'd make her his bride,
   Tho' his flocks and herds were not few,
She gave him her hand, and a kifs befide,
   And vow'd fhe'd forever be true ;
     Bonny Jockey, blyth and free.
     Won her heart right merrily,
At church fhe no more frowning cry'd, no, no, it will
   not do,
I cannot cannot, wonnot wonnot, mannot buckle too.

SONG LXXXVIII.

LULLABY.

Peaceful slumb'ring on the   Ocean, Sailors

fear no danger nigh; The winds and   waves in

gen le motion, Soothe them with their lull a-by.

lul-la-by,   lul-la-by,   lul-la-by,   lul-la by. Soothe

them with   their lul-la - by.

Is the wind tempestuous blowing?
Still no danger they defcry ;
The guilelefs heart its boon bestowing
Soothes them with its lullaby.
    Lullaby, &c.

T 2

When the midnight tempeſt rageing,
  Rolls the angry billows high ;
The morrow's calm their thoughts engaging,
  Soothes them with its lullaby.
    Lullaby, &c.

Now the threat'ning ſtorm is over,
  Clouds no more enſhroud the ſky ;
Blifsful thoughts of abſent lovers,
  Soothe them with their lullaby.
    Lullaby, &c.

The voyage being made, the ſhip's returning,
  Port now greets the raptur'd eye ;
Joy in every boſom burning,
  Soothes them with its lullaby.
    Lullaby, &c.

Safe arriv'd, at anchor riding,
  Hands aſhore all eager fly ;
Happy wives with gentleſt chiding,
  Soothe them with their lullaby.
    Lullaby, &c.

SONG LXXXIX.

THE PRIMROSE GIRL.

Come buy of poor Kate, primroses I sell;

In London's fam'd city I'm known very well,

Tho'my heart is quite sad, yet I constantly

cry, Primroses, primroses, who'll buy my

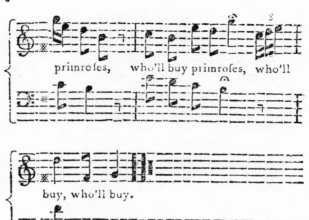

primrofes,   who'll buy primrofes,   who'll

buy, who'll buy.

Relations I've none, I'm look'd on with fcorn,
'Twere better for me had I never been born ;
Though poor, I am honeft, yet oft do I figh,
When crying primrofes, who'll buy my primrofes, &c.

By the rich, and the proud, I am turn'd out of door,
And denied a fmall portion of food from their ftore ;
Unpitied, and hungry, with tears in my eye,
I ftill cry primrofes, who'll buy my primrofes, &c.

My companions all fhun me, and fay I am proud,
Becaufe I avoid them, and keep from their crowd ;
All wicked temptations I ever will fly,
And cry my primrofes, who'll buy my primrofes, &c.

My drefs is quite plain, and my parentage low,
By the world I'm derided wherever I go ;
Yet in fpite of derifion I conftantly cry,
Primrofes, primrofes, who'll buy my primrofes, &c.

Each morn when I wake, to my tafk I repair,
And felect my primrofes, 'tween hope and defpair ;
If I fell them I feaft, but if not, O ! I figh,
  O'er my wither'd primrofer, neglected primrofes,
Poor drooping primrofes, who'll buy, who'll buy ?

And when the day's paft, whether hungry or fed,
From my tafk I retire, to procure me a bed ;
But too often, in forrow, on the cold ground I lie,
  Weeping o'er my primrofes, poor fading primrofes
Neglected primrofes, who'll buy, who'll buy ?

If pity to virtue was ever allied,
The tear of compaffion cannot be denied ;
Then pity poor Kate, who does conftantly cry,
Primrofes, primrofes, who'll buy my primrofes, &c.

SONG XC.

LOVELY STELLA.

Sym. flow.

Bright Sol at length by Thetis woo'd, Is funk beneath the western flood; And now within yon fac - red

grove; I haſte to meet, I haſte to meet

the youth I love.

Sym.

Reclin'd beneath the beachen ſhade, While

zephyrs whiſper round his head, Methinks I

hear him figh - ing fay, Come lovely Stella,

Come lovely, Stella, Come lovely Stel-la,

come a - way.

I come my Damon, fraught with joy ;
Swift as the mountain deer I fly,
Within thy faithful arms to lay,
And love the cares of life away.
There will I vow dear gen'rous youth,
To love thee with eternal truth ;
Firm as great Heav'n's unchang'd decree,
To keep my fpotlefs heart for thee.

By that fond heart, the trueft, beft,
That ever warm'd a Virgin's breaft ,
By that fond heart, dear youth, I fwear,
Thou, only Thou, art treafur'd there :
There fhalt thou ever, deareft fwain,
My bofom's faithful inmate reign !
While oft I'll fay, which all muft fee,
Was ever woman bleft like me ?

SONG XCI.

THE INDIAN PHILOSOPHER.

Why fhould our joys transform to pain ? Why

U

In vain I fought the wond'rous caufe,
Rang'd the wide fields of nature's laws,
 And urg'd the fchools in vain ;
Then deep in thought, within my breaft,
My foul retir'd and flumber drefs'd
 A bright inftructive fcene.

O'er the broad lands, and crofs the tide ;
On fancy's airy horfe I ride,
 (Sweet rapture of the mind !)
'Till on the banks of *Gange*'s flood,
In a tall ancient grove I ftood
 For facred ufe defign'd.

Hard by a venerable prieft,
Ris'n with his God, the Sun, from reft,
 Awoke his morning fong !
Thrice he conjur'd the murm'ring ftream ;
The birth of fouls was all his theme,
 And half divine his tongue.

" He fang th'Eternal rolling flame,
" That vital mafs, which ftill the fame
 " Does all our minds compofe :
" But fhap'd in twice ten thoufand frames
" Thence diff'ring fouls of diff'ring names,
 " And jarring tempers rofe.

" The mighty power which form'd the mind
" One mould for ev'ry two defign'd,
 " And blefs'd the new-born pair :

" *This be a match for that ;* (he faid)
" Then down he fent the fouls he made,
    " To feek them bodies here :

" But parting from their warm abode
" They loft their fellows on the road,
    " And never join'd their hands :
" Ah cruel chance, and croffing fates !
" Our *Eaftern* fouls have dropt their mates
    " On *Europe's* barb'rous lands.

" Happy the youth who finds the Bride,
" Whofe birth is to his own ally'd,
    " The fweeteft joys of life :
" But oh the crowds of wretched fouls
" Fetter'd to minds of diff'rent moulds,
    " And chain'd t' eternal ftrife !

Thus fang the wond'rous *Indian* bard ;
My foul with vaft attention heard,
    While *Ganges* ceas'd to flow :
" Sure then (I cri'd) might I but fee
" That gentle nymph who twin'd with me,
    " I may be happy too.

" Some courteous angel, tell me where,
" What diftant lands this unknown fair,
    " Or diftant feas detain ?
" Swift as the wheel of nature rolls
" I'd fly to meet, and mingle fouls,
    " And wear the joyful chain.

SONG XCII.

THE LIFE OF A BEAU.

Lively.

How brimful of nothing's the life of a

beau, They've noth - ing to think of they've

nothing to do, And nothing to talk of, for

CHORUS.

nothing they know; Such, such is the life of a

U 2

beau. Such, fuch is the life of a beau.

For nothing they rife, but to draw the frefh air,
Spend the morning in nothing but curling their hair,
And do nothing all day, but fing, faunter and ftare.
    Such, fuch is the life of a beau !

For nothing at night to the playhoufe they croud,
To mind nothing done there, they are always too proud,
But to bow and to grin and to talk nothing loud.
    Such, fuch is the life of a beau !

For nothing they run to affembly and ball,
And for nothing at cards a fair partner they call,
For they ftill muft be *hafted* who've nothing at all.
    Such, fuch is the life of a beau !

For nothing on Sundays at church they appear,
They have nothing to hope for and nothing to fear,
They can be nothing no where, who nothing are here.
    Such, fuch is the life of a beau !

SONG XCIII.

A NEW SONG, FOR A SERENADE—By D. GEORGE.

Andante.

Rise, my Delia, heav'nly charmer, Deign my

passion to ap - prove. Musick! of her

pride dif - arm her, Melt her heart with notes of

love. Musick! of her pride dif-arm her, Melt

her heart with notes of   love.

Cynthia from the eaſt aſcending,
    Sheds her beauties on the night ;
And the glitt'ring ſtars attending,
    Aid me with their feeble light.

Gentle zephyrs, ſoftly blowing,
    Seem to whiſper tales of love :
Sweeteſt notes in muſic flowing---
    O ! could they my Delia move !

Pearly dew drops, that ſuſpended
    On the flowr's, my anguiſh ſpeak ;
Like my tears, as they deſcended
    Down my fading, pallid cheek.

Balmy ſleep o'er anture hovers,
    With his black impervious wings ;
Yet to ever watchful lovers,
    Silent night no ſolace brings.

Why this wiſhing---trembling---dying---
    This fond hope, and tender fear ?
Friendly zephyrs, dovelike flying,
    Waft my ſighs to Delia's ear !

Tell her that for her I languish---
  What each tender look reveals ;
Fill her bosom with soft anguish ;
  Teach her what her lover feels.

Smile propitious, heav'nly creature,
  Ease my love sick, painful breast :
'Tis not in my Delia's nature
  To deprive my soul of rest.

SONG XCIV.

FRIENDSHIP—By *BIDWELL.*

Friendship to   ev'ry willing mind Opens a

heav'nly treasure : There may the sons of

row find Sources of re - al   pleafure. See

what employments men purfue, Then you will

own my words are true: Friendfhip a-lone un-

folds to view Sources of re - al pleafure.

Poor are the joys which fools efteem,
  Fading and tranfitory :
Mirth is as fleeting as a dream,
  Or a delufive ftory :
Luxury leaves a fting behind,
Wounding the body and the mind :
Only in Friendfhip can we find
  Pleafure and folid glory,

Beauty, with all its gaudy fhows,
  Is but a painted bubble :
Short is the triumph, wit beftows,
  Full of deceit and trouble :
Fame, like a fhadow, flees away,
Titles and dignities decay :
Nothing but Friendfhip can difplay
  Joys, that are free form trouble.

Learning (that boafted glittering thing)
  Scarcely is worth poffeffing :
Riches, forever on the wing,
  Cannot be call'd a bleffing :
Senfual pleafures fwell defire,
Juft as the fuel feeds the fire :
Friendfhip can real blifs infpire,
  Blifs that is worth poffeffing,

Happy the man, who has a friend
  Form'd by the God of nature,
Well may he feel and recommend
  Friendfhip for his Creator.

Then as our hands in Friendſhip join,
So let our ſocial powers combine,
Rul'd by a paſſion moſt divine,
Friendſhip with our Creator.

SONG XCV.
NOBODY.

If to force me to ſing it   be yonr intention,

Some one I will hint at, yet nobody mention,

Nobody   you'll cry, pſhaw, that muſt be ſtuff,

At   ſinging I'm no-bo-dy, that's the firſt proof,

No, no-bo-dy,   no, no-bo-dy,   no-bo-dy,

nobody,   no-bo-dy, no.

Nobody's a name every body will own,
When fomething they ought to be afham'd of have
    done ;
'Tis a name well applied to old maids and young beaus,
What they were intended for nobody knows.
        No, nobody, &c.

If negligent fervants fhould china-plate crack,
The fault is ftill laid on poor nobody's back ;
If accidents happen at home or abroad,
When nobody's blam'd for it, is not that odd ?
        No, nobody &c.

Nobody can tell you the tricks that are play'd,
When nobody's by, betwixt mafter and maid :
She gently crys out, fir, there'll fome body hear us,
He foftly replies, my dear, nobody's near us.
        No, nobody, &c.

But big with child proving, fhe's quickly difcarded,
When favours are granted, nobody's rewarded ;
And when fhe's examined, crys, mortals, forbid it,
If I'm got with child, it was nobody did it.
        No, nobody, &c.

When by ftealth, the gallant, the wanton wife leaves,
The hufband's affrighten'd, and thinks it is thieves ;
He roufes himfelf, and crys loudly who's there ?
The wife pats his cheek, and fays, nobody, dear.
        No, nobody, &c.
            W

Enough now of nobody fure has been fung,
Since nobody's mention'd, nor nobody's wrong'd;
I hope for free fpeaking I may not be blam'd,
Since nobody's injur'd, nor nobody's nam'd.
No, nobody, &c.

SONG XCVI.

THE DISPAIRING DAMSEL.

'Twas when the feas were roaring With hollow blafts of wind; A damfel lay deploring, All on a rock reclin'd. Wide o'er the foaming billows She caft a wiftful look; Her head was crown'd with willows That trembled o'er the brook.

Twelve months are gone and over,
  And nine long tedious days :
Why didſt thou vent'rous lover,
  Why didſt thou truſt the ſeas ?
Ceaſe, ceaſe, thou cruel ocean,
  And let my lover reſt :
Ah ! what's thy troubled motion
  To that within my breaſt.

The merchant, robb'd of treaſure,
  Views tempeſts in deſpair ;
But what's the loſs of treaſure
  To loſing of my dear !
Should you ſome coaſt be laid on,
  Where gold and di'monds grow,
You'd find a richer maiden,
  But none that loves you ſo.

How can they ſay that nature
  Has nothing made in vain ;
Why then beneath the water
  Do hideous rocks remain ;
No eyes theſe rocks diſcover,
  That lurk beneath the deep,
To wreck the wand'ring lover,
  And leave the maid to weep.

All melancholy lying,
  Thus wail'd ſhe for her dear ;
Repaid each blaſt with ſighing,
  Each billow with a tear :

When o'er the white wave ſtooping,
His floating corpſe ſhe ſpied :
Then, like a lily, drooping,
She bow'd her head, and died.

SONG XCVII.

DEATH OR VICTORY.

ANDANTIO.

Hark, the din of diſtant war, How no-

ble is the clangor; Pale death aſcends his

E - bon car, Clad in ter - rif - ic an -

ger. A doubtful fate the foldier tries, Who

joins the gal-lant quar - rel. Per-haps on

the cold ground he lies, No wife, no friend

to clofe his eyes, Though nobly mourn'd, per-

haps return'd, He's crown'd with vict'ry's

law - rel.

How many who difdaining fear,
  Rufh on the defp'rate duty ;
Shall claim the tribute of the tear,
  That dims the eye of beauty.

A doubtful fate, the foldier tries,
  Who joins the gallant quarrel.
Perheps on the cold ground he lies,
No wife, no friend to clofe his eyes :
Tho' nobly mourn'd, perhaps return'd,
  He's crown'd with vict'ry's lawrel,

W 2

What nobler fate can fortune give ?
Renown fhall tell our ftory
If we fhould fall ; but if we live,.
We live our country's glory.

'Tis true a doubtful fate he tries,
   Who joins the gallant quarrel.
Perhaps on the cold ground he lies,
No wife, no friend to clofe his eyes .
Tho' nobly mourn'd, perhaps return'd,
   He's crown'd with vict'ry's lawrel.

SONG XCVIII.

OH ! SAY SIMPLE MAID.

A Duet, in the Comic Opera of INCLE and YARICO.

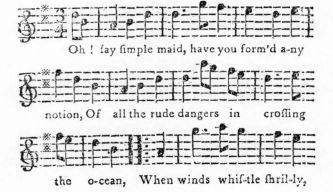

Oh ! fay fimple maid, have you form'd a-ny

notion, Of all the rude dangers in croffing

the o-cean, When winds whif-tle fhril-ly,

ah! wou'd they remind you, To figh with re-

gret for the grot left be-hind you.

YARICO.

Ah no, I could follow and fail the world over,
Nor think of my grot when I look at my lover ;
The winds that blow round us, your arms for my pillow,
Will lull us to fleep, while we're rock'd by each billow.

INKLE.

Then fay lovely lafs, what if haply efpying,
A rich gallant veffel, with gay colours flying ?

YARICO.

I'll journey with thee love, to where the land narrows,
And fling all my cares at my back, with my arrows.

BOTH.

O fay then, my true love, we never will funder,
Nor fhrink from the tempeft, nor dread the big thunder ;
Still conftant, I'll laugh at all changes of weather,
And journey all over the world both together.

SONG XCIX.

TOM TACKLE.

ANDANTINO.

Tom Tackle was no-ble, was true to his word,

If merit bought   titles, Tom might be my

lord : How gayly his bark thro' life's ocean

wou'd fail, Truth furnifh'd the rigging, and

honour the gale : Yet Tom had a failing, if

ever man had, That good as he was, made him

all that was bad ; He was paltry and pitiful,

scurvy and mean, And the sniv'-ling-eft scoundrel

that ev - er was seen : For so said the girls

and the landlords long shore, Wou'd you know what

this fault was, Tom Tackle was poor, Tom

Tackle was poor. was poor, Tom Tackle was

poor, Wou'd you know what this fault was,

Tom   Tackle was   poor.

'Twas once on a time, when we took a galleon,
And the crew touch'd the agent for cafh, to fome tune ;
Tom a trip took to prifon, an old mefsmate to free,
And four thankful pratlers foon fat on each knee :
Then Tom was an angel, downright from heav'n fent,
While they'd hands, he his goodnefs fhou'd never
     repent,
Return'd from next voyage, he bemoan'd his hard cafe,
To find his dear friend, fhut the door in his face
Why d'ye wonder, cried one, you'r ferv'd right to be
     fure,
Once Tom Tackle was rich, now Tom Tackle is poor.

I be'nt you fee, vers'd in high maxims and fich,
But don't this fame honour concern poor and rich,
If it don't come from good hearts, I can't fee where from,
And damme if e'er tar had good heart 'twas Tom :
Yet fomehow or other, Tom never did right,
None knew better the time when to fpare or to fight :
He by finding a leak, once preferv'd crew and fhip,
Sav'd the commodres life—Then he made fuch rare flip,
And yet for all this, no one Tom coul'd endure,
I fancy as how 'twas becaufe he was poor.

At laft an old fhipmate that Tom might hail land,
Who faw that his heart fail'd too faft for his hand,

In the riding of comfort, a mooring to find,
Reef'd the fails of Toms fortune, that fhook in the wind ;
He gave him enough thro' life's ocean to fteer,
Be the breeze what it may, fteady, thus or too near.
His pittance is daily, and yet Tom imparts,
What he can to his friends.--And may all honeft hearts,
Like Tom Tackle, have what keeps the wolf from
        the door,
Juft enough to be gen'rous, too much to be poor.

SONG C.

THE CHARMS OF NATURE.

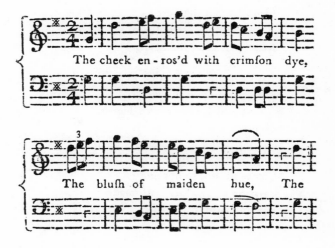

The cheek en - ros'd with crimfon dye,

The blufh of maiden hue,   The

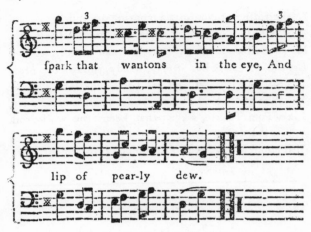

spark that   wantons   in   the eye, And

lip of   pear-ly   dew.

To man thefe native charms appear
    More elegant than art ;
The painted fiufh—the fnareful leer—
    Ne'er penetrate the heart.

What boots the bloom that pencil lays
    Each morn upon the face ?
Can that which ere the eve decays,
    Be juftly deem'd a grace ?

The nymph who trufts to nature's aid,
    Comes neareft to her end ;
For nature ne'er a face hath made,
    For human fkill to mend.

SONG CI.

POLLY PLY.

ALLEGRO.

If ev-er a iailor was fond of good

fport 'Mongft the girls, why that fail-or was I:

Of all fiz-es and forts, I'd a wife at each port;

But when that I faw'd Pol-ly Ply, I

hail'd her my lovely, and gov'd her a kifs, And

fwore to bring up once for all, And from that

time Black Bar-na-by fplic'd us 'till this, from

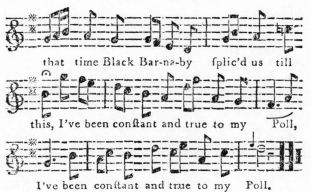

that time Black Bar-na-by   fplic'd us   till

this, I've been conftant and true to my   Poll,

I've been conftant and true to my   Poll.

And yet now all forts of temptations I've ftood,
    For I afterwards fail'd round the world,
And a queer fet we faw of the devils own brood,
    Wherever our fails were unfurl'd ;
Some with faces like charcoal and others like chalk,
    All ready one's heart to o'erhall,
Don't ye go to love me my good girl's faid I walk,
    I've fworn to be conftant to Poll.

I met with a fquaw, out at India beyond,
    All in glafs and tobacco pipes dreft,
What a dear pretty monfter ! fo kind and fo fond,
    That I ne'er was a moment at reft ;
With her bobs at her nofe, & her quaw, quaw, quaw,
    All the world like a Bartle, my Doll,
Says I you mifs copperfkin, juft hold your jaw,
    For I fhall be conftant to Poll.

Then one near Sumatra, juſt under the line,
  As fond as a witch in a play,
I loves you, ſays ſhe, and juſt only be mine,
  Or by poiſon I'll take you away ;
Curſe your kindneſs, ſays I, but you ſhan't frighten me,
  You don't catch a gudgeon this haul,
If I do take your rats-bane why then do you ſee,
  I ſhall die true and conſtant to Poll.

But I ſcap'd from'em all, tawny, lily, and black,
  And merrily weather'd each ſtorm,
And my neighbours to pleaſe, full of wonders came back,
  But what's better, I'm grown pretty warm ;
And ſo now to ſea I ſhall ventur no more,
  For you know being rich I've no call,
So I'll bring up young tars, do my duty on ſhore,
  And live and die conſtant to Poll.

SONG CII.

THO' BACCHUS MAY BOAST OF HIS CARE KILLING BOWL.

Tho'   Bacchus may boaft of his care-killing

bowl, And   Folly in thought-drowning revels

delight, Such worfhip a-las ! hath no charms

for the foul, When fofter   devotions the fenfes

invite : When fofter devotions the   fen - fes

invite. To the   arrow of fate, or the   canker

of care, His potions oblivious a balm may be-

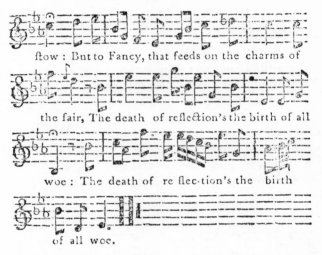

flow : But to Fancy, that feeds on the charms of

the fair, The death of reflection's the birth of all

woe : The death of re flec-tion's the birth

of all woe.

What foul that's poffeft of a dream fo divine,
  With riot would bid the fweet vifion begone ?
For the tear that bedews Senfibility's fhrine
  Is a drop of more worth than all Bacchus's tun.

Is a drop of more worth than all Baccchus's tun.

The tender excefs which enamonrs the heart,
  To few is imparted, to millions deny'd :
'Tis the brain of the victim that tempers the dart,
  And fools jeft at that for which fages have died.
      And fools, &c.

Each change and excefs hath through life been my
    doom,
And well can I fpeak of its joy and its ftrife ;
The bottle affords us a glimpfe thro' the gloom,
    But love's the true funfhine that gladdens our life,
        But love's, &c.

Come, then, rofy Venus, and fpread o'er my fight
    The magic illufions that ravifh the foul :
Awake in my breaft the foft dream of delight,
    And drop from thy myrtle one leaf in my bowl,
        And drop, &c.

Then deep will I drink of the nectar divine,
    Nor e'er, jolly God, from thy banquet remove,
But each tube of my heart ever thirft for the wine,
    That's mellow'd by friendfhip, and fweeten'd by
    love.

That's mellow'd by friendfhip, and fweeten'd by love.

₊ The above Notes are trifling deviations from the original melody, to fuit the expreffion of the different ftanzas.

SONG CIII.

STREW THE SWEET ROSES OF PLEASURE BETWEEN.

Pompofo.

If life's a rough path, as the fages have

faid, With flints and with weeds and with briers

befpread, With flints and with weeds and with

bri-ers be-fpread, When the fcorpions of

en-vy and adders of hate, Conceal'd in clofe

ambufh to wound us a - wait, It fure - ly is

wifdom to foft-en the fcene, By ftrewing the

rofes of pleafure between. It fure - ly is

wifdom to foft-en the fcene, By ftrewing the

rofes of pleafure between.

Yes, nature intended that man fhould be bleft,
Since the focial affeQions fhe thron'd in his breaft ;
And he who morofely would mar her defign,
Deferves in a defert forever to pine ;
Without one gay vifion his foul to ferene,
Or ftrew the fweet rofes of pleafure between.

Then crown me the goblet that fooother of care,
And call wit and beauty the banquet to fhare ;
Bid that o'er my reafon, and this o'er my fenfe,
The charms of their heart touching magick difpenfe ;
To fling o'er life's path a foft carpet of green,
And ftrew the fweet rofes of pleafure between.

SONG CIV.

WASHINGTON.

Set to Music by S. Holyoke.

When Al - ci - des, the fon of O - lym-

pian Jove, Was call'd from the earth to the

regions a - bove, The fetters grim Tyranny

twift from his hand, And with rapine and mur-

der u-furp'd the command; While Peace, lovely

maiden, was fcar'd from the plains, And Liber-

ty, captive, fat wailing in chains; Her

once gallant ofsfpring lay bleeding around,

Nor on earth could a champion to save her be

found. Her once, &c.

Nor on. &c.

The thunderer, mov'd with compaffion, look'd down
On a world fo accurs'd, from his cryftalline throne ;
Then open'd the book, in whofe myftical page
Were enrolled the heroes of each future age ;
Read of Brutus and Sidney, who dar'd to be free,
Of their virtues approv'd, and confirm'd the decree :
Then turn'd to the annals of that happy age,
When Wafhington's glories illumin'd the page.

" When Britannia fhall ftrive with tyrannical hand
" To eftablifh her empire in each diftant land,
" A chief fhall arife, in Columbia's defence,
" To whome the juft Gods fhall their favours difpenfe,
" Triumphant as Mars in the glorious field,
" While Minerva fhall lend him her wifdom and fhield,
" And liberty, freed from her fhackles, fhall own
" Great Wafhington's claim as her favourite fon."

Y

SONG CV.
HOW COLD IT IS!
A WINTER SONG.

See now the bluft'ring Boreas blows,

See all the waters round are froze,   The

trees that fkirt the drea - ry plain All day a

murm'ring cry maintain ; The trembling foreſt

hears their moan, And ſadly mingles groan with

groan. How diſmal all from eaſt to weſt !

May heav'n defend the poor diftreft !   Such

is the   tale,   On hill and vale, Each trav'ler

may behold it   is ;   While low and high

Are heard to cry, Ah ! blefs my heart, how cold

it is ! Ah ! blefs my heart, how cold it is !

Now flumb'ring floth that cannot bear
The queftion of the fearching air,
Lifts up her unkempt head and tries,
But cannot from her bondage rife ;
The whilft the houfe wife brifkly throws
Around her wheel, and fweetly fhows
The healthful cheek induftry brings,
Which is not in the gift of kings.
     To her, long life
      Devoid of ftrife,
       Y 2

And juſtly too, unfolded is ;
    The whilſt the ſloth
    To ſtir is loth
And trembling cries, how cold it is ?

Now liſps Sir Fopling, tender weed ?
All ſhiv'ring like a ſhaken reed !
How keen the air attacks my back !
John place ſome liſt upon that crack ;
Go ſand-bag all the ſaſhes round,
And ſee there's not an air hole found.
Ah ! bleſs me, now I feel a breath,
Good lack ! 'tis like the chill of death.
    Indulgence pale
    Tells this ſad tale,
Till he in furs infolded is ;
    Still, ſtill complains
    For all his pains,
Ah ! bleſs my heart, how cold it is !

Now the poor newſman from the town,
Explores his path along the down,
His frozen fingers ſadly blows,
And ſtill he ſeeks, and ſtill it ſnows ;
Till cover'd all from head to feet,
Like penance in her whiteſt ſheet.
Go take his paper, Richard, go,
And give a dram to make him glow.

    This was thy cry,
    Humanity.
More precious far than gold it is,
    Such gifts to deal
    When newfmen feel,
All clad in fnow, how cold it is!

Humanity, delightful tale!
While we all feel the wintry gale,
O may the cit in ermin'd coat
Incline the ear to forrow's note;
And where, with mis'ry's weight oppreft,
A fellow fits a fhiv'ring gueft,
Full ample let his bounty flow
To foothe the bofom chill'd by woe;
    In town or vale,
    Where'er the tale
Of real grief, unfolded is,
    O may he give
    The means to live,
To thofe who know, how cold it is!

Perhaps fome warriour, blind and lam'd,
Some tar, for independence maim'd,
Confider thefe, for thee they bore
The lofs of limb, and fuffer'd more:
O pafs them not, or if you do,
I'll figh to think they fought for you.

Go pity all, but 'bove the reft.
The foldier or the tar diftrefs'd :
    Thro' winter's reign
    Relieve their pain.
For what they've done, fure bold it is :
    Their wants fupply,
    Whene'er they cry
Ah! blefs my heart, how cold it is!

And now ye fluggards, floths, and beaux,
Who dread the breath that winter blows,
Purfue the counfel of a friend
Who never found it yet offend ;
While Winter deals his froft around,
Go face the air, and beat the ground,
With cheerful fpirits exercife,
'Tis there life's balmy blefling lies :
    On hill and dale.
    Tho' fharp the gale
And frozen you behold it is,
    The blood fhall glow,
    And fweetly flow,
And you'll ne'er cry, how cold it is !

SONG CVI.

A SHAPE ALONE LET OTHERS PRIZE.

Set to Music by H. GRAM.

Expressively.

shape a - lone let   oth - ers prize, And fea-

tures of the   fair,   I   look for   spirit

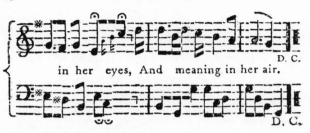

in her   eyes,   And   meaning in her air.

D. C.

D. C.

A damaſk cheek, an iv'ry arm,
  Shall ne'er my wiſhes win,
Give me an animated form,
  That ſpeaks a mind within.

A ſoul where awful honour ſhines,
  Where ſenſe and ſweetneſs move,
And angel innocence refines,
  The tenderneſs of love.

With pow'r to heighten ev'ry joy,
  The fierceſt rage control,
Diffuſing mildneſs o'er the brow,
  And raptures thro' the ſoul.

Theſe are the pow'rs of beauty's charms,
  Without whoſe vital aid,
Unfiniſh'd all her beauty ſeems,
  And all her roſes dead.

But how divinely ſhines the form,
  Where all theſe charms appear,
Then go behold my *Anna's* face,
  And read them perfect there.

SONG CVII.

BRIGHT DAWNS THE DAY ;
A HUNTING SONG.

Set to Music by a Student of the University at Cambridge.

RECITATIVE.

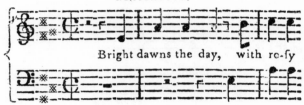

Bright dawns the day, with ro-fy

face, That calls the hunter to the chace.

Adagio.

With mu-fic-al horn fa-lute the gay morn,

These jol-ly com-pan-ions to cheer. With en-

liv'ning founds, encourage the hounds, To

ri-val the fpeed of the de - - - - - - er. To

ri-val the fpeed   of   the   deer.

SONG.—Verse I.

If you find out his lair, To the wood-

lands re-pair; Hark! hark! he's un-harbour'd

they cry; Then fleet o'er the plain, We'll

gal-lop a - main, All, all is a

Z

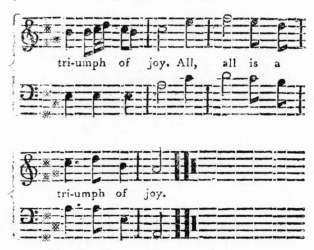

tri-umph of joy. All, all is a

tri-umph of joy.

Over heaths, hills and woods,
Thro' the forefts and floods,
The ftag flies as fwift as the wind ;
The welkin refounds
With the cry of the hounds,
That chaunt in a chorus behind.

Then adieu to old Care,
To pale Grief and Defpair,
We ride in oblivion of fear ;
Vexation and pain
We leave to the train,
Sad wretches, who lag in the rear.

Lo ! the ftag ftands at bay,
And the pack's at a ftay ;
Then eagerly feize on the prize ;
The welkin refounds
With the chorus of hounds,
Shrill horns wind his knell, and he dies !

SONG CVIII.

WINTER.

A-dieu, ye groves, a-dieu ye plains, All na-

ture mourning lies. See gloomy clouds, and

thick'ning rains Obfcure the lab'ring fkies.

See, fee, from a-far, th'im-pend-ing ftorm With

fullen hafte ap-pear, See win-ter comes, A

dreary form, to rule - - - the falling year.

No more the lambs with gamefome bound,
   Rejoice the gladden'd fight :
No more the gay enamell'd ground,
   Or fylvan fcenes delight.
Thus, lovely Nancy, much lov'd maid,
   Thy early charms muft fail ;
Thy rofe muft droop, the lily fade,
   And winter foon prevail,

Again the lark, fweet bird of day,
   May rife on active wings,
Again the fportive herds may play,
   And hail reviving fpring,
But youth, my fair, fees no return,
   The pleafing bubble's o'er,
In vain it's fleeting joys you mourn,
   They fall to bloom no more.

Hafte, then dear girl, the time improve,
   Which art can ne'er regain,
In blifsfull fcenes of mutual love,
   With fome diftinguifh'd fwain ;
So fhall life's fpring, like jocund May,
   Pafs fmiling and ferene ;
Thus fummer, autumn, glide away,
   And winter foon prevail.

SONG CIX.

SONG IN THE SPOIL'D CHILD.

Since then I'm doom'd this fad reverfe to prove,

To quit each ob-ject   of my in-fant care ;

Torn from an honour'd parent's tender love, And

driv'n the keen-eft   ftorms   of   fate   to

bear: Ah! but for-give me, oh! piti'd let me

part, Your frowns too   fure, wou'd break my

finking heart.   Ah! but for - give me, oh!
Z 2

piti'd　let me　part, Your　frowns　too　　　fure

wou'd　break　my　finking　heart.

Oft have you faid I was your only joy,
Ah ! wretch to forfeit fuch an envied blifs !
You too have deign'd to call me darling boy,
And own'd your fondnefs with a mother's kifs.
Ah ! then forgive me, piti'd let me part,
Your frowns too fure wou'd break my finking heart.

Where'er I go, whate'er my lowly ftate,
Yet grateful mem'ry ftill fhall linger here !
Perhaps when mufing o'er my cruel fate,
You ftill may greet me with a tender tear.
Ah ! then forgive me, piti'd let me part,
Your frowns too fure, wou'd break my finking heart.

SONG CX.

YE MORTALS WHOM FANCIES.

Ye mortals whom fancies and troubles per-

plex, Whom folly misguides, and infirmities vex,

Whose lives hardly know what it is to be blest,

Who rise without joy, and lie down without rest,

Obey the glad summons, to Lethe re-pair, Drink

deep of the stream, and forget all your care, Drink

deep of the ftream, and forget all your care.

Old maids fhall forget what they wifh for ia vain.
And young ones the rover they cannot regain ;
The rake fhall forget how laft night he was cloy'd,
And Chloe again be with paffion enjoy'd :
Obey then the fummons, to Lethe repair,
And drink an Oblivion to trouble and care.

The wife at one draught, may forget all her wants,
Or drench her fond fool, to forget her gallants ;
The troubled in mind fhall go cheerful away,
And yefterday's wretch be quite happy to day :
Obey then the fummons, to Lethe repair,
Drink deep of the ftream and forget all your care,

SONG CXI.

ON MUSIC.

Largo.

To mu-fic be the verfe ad-

dreſt; To mu-fic, foft - ner of the

breaſt, And what from woe re-lieves; from

woe re - - lieves; 'Tis music, 'Tis

music, like the Sy-ren's charms, With tend'-

reft love the bo - som warms, With

tend'-reft love the bo - - - fom warms,

But not like them de-ceives.

'Tis this the human heart infpires,
With tender feelings, foft defires,
And pleafes ev'ry ear :
'Twas practis'd in the Courts of Jove,
And given by the gods above,
To man, to banish care.

Yet not to man alone, was giv'n
This nobleft, choiceft gift of heav'n,

'Twas taught the feather'd choir ;
The feather'd choir the boon receiv'd,
And quick all Nature was reliev'd,
    For mufic fill'd the air.

When fmiling Spring, with fragrant gales
Perfumes the woodlands, hills and dales ;
    When Nature's charms adorn
With livelieft colours, gentle May,
Tis then the fky lark tunes her lay,
    And ufhers in the morn,

Though not a fragrant gale that blows,
Nor all the beauties May beftows,
    With mufic can compare :
Yet when together thefe combine,
They form on earth a fcene divine—
    A fcene divinely fair.

'Tis this infpires to noble deeds ;
Urg'd on by this, the hero bleeds,
    Nor thinks his lot fevere.
It calms our fears in war's alarms,
And adds to gentler peace new charms—
    Mufic the gods revere.

F I N I S.